# NORTHAMPTONS

# NORTHAMPTONSHIRE MURDERS

## Paul Harrison

COUNTRYSIDE BOOKS
NEWBURY, BERKSHIRE

COUNTRYSIDE BOOKS
3 Catherine Road
Newbury, Berkshire

ISBN 1 85306 147 6


Produced through MRM Associates Ltd, Reading
Typeset by Acorn Bookwork, Salisbury
Printed by J W Arrowsmith Ltd, Bristol

For LESLEY

Elizabeth Fawson, burnt at the stake in 1735 for poisoning her husband. Detail taken from a contemporary broadsheet.

# Contents

# WITH MALICE AFORETHOUGHT

**M**URDER, the unlawful killing of one human being by another is, whichever way you look at it, an emotive subject. It is an irrefutable fact of life that we all enjoy a good murder, not in the physical sense you understand, but as objective outsiders. If you disagree with this claim then perhaps you should recall just how many of those television amateur detective programmes you take in. Like it or not, murder has forced itself upon society and is an accepted part of life (or death). However, unlike the television dramas which tend to glamourise this heinous act, murder is generally a straightforward affair with the victim knowing his/her attacker in an area in which the investigating authorities examine initially.

The county of Northamptonshire is not renowned for its murderous and secret history yet there is a dark and evil past which is quite often forgotten and excluded from written documents on the county. Just why this should be so I do not know. Historically, the county is famous for its industry. The boot and shoe trade prospered within the county for many decades providing sufficient financial remuneration to enable the whole area to expand into a highly industrious community. Apart from the boot and shoe industry the county is perhaps best known for a battle which took place within its confines. In 1645 the decisive battle of Naseby took place between the troops of King Charles I led by Sir Thomas Fairfax, whose strategical knowledge was highly respected, and the aggressive Oliver Cromwell who was at that time Lieutenant-General of the Horse. The Parliamentarians won the day due to Cromwell's battle plan.

Relatively speaking thereafter the county has led an almost quiet unassuming part in English history and apart from the great fire of 1675 which is well documented, there is little else of any great notoriety. Perhaps one incident which caused the county to recoil in horror was the assassination of Prime Minister Spencer Perceval in the lobby of the House of Commons on May 11th 1812. The Right Honourable gentleman, First Lord of the Treasury, was MP for Northampton and had resided within the town. Perceval was murdered by a mentally disturbed man by the name of John Bellingham who blamed the Prime Minister for what he believed was a miscarriage of justice which he had suffered in Russia. Bellingham had plagued Parliament with letters of complaint seeking some form of reimbursement. In the main these missives were ignored but due to their quantity were eventually investigated. The British authorities scrutinised Bellingham's case and decided that there was no cause for complaint as all Bellingham's problems were self induced. John Bellingham became a bitter and twisted man and placed the blame upon Perceval – hence his assassination. At the subsequent trial Bellingham was found guilty of murder and hanged at Newgate. Unfortunately for Bellingham little thought was given to his state of mind. He was obviously suffering from some mental disability but there was no provision in English law for what we now know as 'diminished responsibilities'. This facet of the judicial system did not come into being until 1843, 31 years too late for Bellingham.

In 1324 the 'magistrate' system was introduced by statute; 'within every county there shall be assigned a good and lawful man to keep the peace', and this was the basis around which today's police forces were formed. In 1361 the Justice of the Peace

Act determined and identified powers. Magistrates were selected rather then elected, and the authority given to this individual covered a wide area, from collecting taxes right through to dealing with offenders with their own justice! The magistrates eventually were able to nominate and select subordinates (parish constables) who were really only there to carry out the magistrates' dirty work. These unfortunate individuals received no payment for their duties which they were forced to carry out in their private time. The parish constable was elected annually from the local community. It most certainly was not a coveted position. Prisoners had to be held in the constable's own home until the quarter sessions was held by a local magistrate! This of course included the feeding and general welfare of the individual and again no compensation was awarded to the officer.

By 1836 the basis of the local police and judicial system had hardly altered, though London had seen police constables walking its streets in a designated and uniformed fashion since Sir Robert Peel's act was passed through Parliament. In line with this, 1836 saw the inception of Northamptonshire's Borough police forces which were divided into the various local areas. In 1839 the County Police Act allowed local areas to adapt their police forces to meet with local legislation as well as national rulings and at last a feasible policing system had been produced and established. The initial problem each county encountered was the fact that one individual (titled a Chief Constable) had to be selected from a list of volunteers who in turn had to meet with a set criteria which was different to today's standards. March 1840 saw advertisements placed in the *Northampton Mercury* newspaper. Four separate dates saw a total of 22 applicants, of whom nine were of a service background (Army officers), and just four were able to quote any police experience as such. The salary for the Chief Constable was quoted at £250 per annum which was quite a reasonable sum at that time, hence the high standard of social class of those who applied for the position.

Among those who applied was one Henry Goddard, a plain clothes detective with the Bow Street Runners since 1826. Within the decade which followed Goddard had become accepted as being one of the top detectives (as such) within the United Kingdom. The Runners had disbanded in 1839, forcing Goddard to find some other form of employment. Using his investigating skills to best effect Goddard took a position as a private detective and it was from this occupation that Goddard was given the historical position of first Chief Constable of Northamptonshire. Goddard altered very little in his nine years in office, though he did split the county into various policing divisions.

In 1849 Goddard was replaced by Henry Lambart Bayly, whose background differed greatly to that of his predecessor. Rather than opting for experience, the magistrates went for social standing. Bayly was the son of Irish gentry, though to be fair he had some limited experience in the Irish Constabulary. Yet during his term of office Henry Bayly altered the basis of the force drastically. The changes were far ahead of their time and some of them remained in being for well over a century. The election of Bayly as Chief Constable was an inspired selection by the magistrates, who obviously realised the man's potential during application interviews.

Bayly resigned from the force in June 1875 and was replaced by Charles Pearson, the then Chief Constable of Caernarfonshire. Pearson had a large family and household staff and did not like the accommodation away from Northampton town centre. He was advised that his residence would be required to be within one mile of the town centre. Pearson remonstrated and told the magistrates that other Chiefs in similar positions resided up to five miles away from their county towns. The magistrates were adamant that Pearson should live within the one mile boundary so Pearson resigned after just three hours in office!

After a quick readjustment the magistrates elected Thomas Orde Hastings Lees as new Chief Constable. Lees was from a similar background to Henry Bayly and one must assume that the authorities were keen to see someone of a similar disposition as Bayly in power. Unfortunately Lees offered little new but maintained the status quo during his tenure. He was politically competent and promoted the force at every opportunity, as one would expect from a qualified barrister.

Lees was unfortunate enough to be in the post when an horrific accident occurred on the Northampton to Wellingborough railway line close to Little Houghton. A train travelling towards Wellingborough containing numerous persons who had been present at the Northampton quarter sessions earlier that day, was struck by a ballast train. The screams of agony and the squeal of stressed metal twisting and bending were heard for miles around. Gushing steam rose into the night air like a great tree towering above the twisted wreckage of the two trains. Great bonfires were lit alongside the scene of carnage in order to illuminate the site for rescuers. Passengers were found on the line with broken legs and suffering from shock and Police Superintendent Lewis Poole was found dead – almost decapitated by one of the wheels of the ballast train. Police Sergeant Isaac Wilson of Kettering had been thrown onto the line and beneath the wheels, necessitating the amputation of his right leg. Sadly Wilson died the following day. A journalist by the name of William Leatherland of the *Wellingborough News* also died by virtue of injuries received, as too did Police Constable Thomas Barrett of Rothwell, who was so badly injured that it was an almost impossible task to remove him from the wreckage without causing immediate death. It was a black few days for the county police for each of the men had been popular figures within their own right. Local communities mourned as too did every serving police officer in the county. Two persons were brought before the Northampton assizes charged with the manslaughter of those killed in the crash.

James Gibson, a railway inspector, and Thomas Gardener, a signalman, found themselves bearing the brunt of public and official condemnation. It was Gardener whose position came under closest scrutiny as it was he who allowed the ballast train onto the stretch of track on which the oncoming passenger train was travelling. Various discrepancies came to light. Gardener had been a signalman for just three months while Gibson claimed to have acted as efficiently as anyone could under the circumstances. The jury heard all the evidence and must have been somewhat concerned by the facts of the case. However, they erred on the side of caution and reached a verdict of 'not guilty' on both men. Whatever the verdict, it was a bleak October in 1877 which will never truly be forgotten.

Thomas Orde Hasting Lees was followed as Chief Constable by James Dalgleish Kellie-McCallum who is remembered for different reasons, primarily due to the fact that he is recorded as being the longest serving Chief Constable of any county police force (1881–1931). McCallum was an amazing 85 years of age when he retired from Northamptonshire Police on 1st June 1931. This was due to a discrepancy in the hard-fought Police Pensions Acts of 1890 and 1921 which failed to compensate for a certain criterion which McCallum fitted. Of all the senior officials the force has had, McCallum is recalled as being the most correct from a welfare point of view. It is claimed that he could individually identify every officer within the force, discussing personal details in some depth!

During his term of office he saw two generations of police officers come and go and also saw great changes within the force, especially in the way in which offenders were apprehended. This was illustrated when in April 1899 the circus arrived in Northampton, always a special event, especially for the younger generation. The circus and all of its entertainers were welcome guests wherever they visited. Under most circumstances this was quite acceptable. However, the circus, like all other high profile activities, had its fair share of problems, especially with those who indiscriminately abused its power for their own gain. Frederick John Phillips was one such entrepreneur. Phillips printed some bogus complimentary tickets for the future 'Barnum and Bailey' circus in the town. Three shops were visited on the outskirts of Northampton, one each at Far Cotton, Duston and Dallington. Each shop was owned by a woman, who Phillips obviously saw as easy prey. Phillips explained to each shopkeeper that he was an advance publicity agent for the circus and advised his gullible clients that he would provide them with free tickets in return for placing a publicity poster about the forthcoming circus in their window. He went on to explain that although the tickets were free it was usual practice to pay him a little something in advance. Each shopkeeper fell for his patter and gave the imposter some financial compensation for his apparent kindness. Only when he was gone did they realise they had been tricked!

Normally such incidents would remain unsolved as the imposter generally left the area without being found out. However, the shopkeeper from Dallington heard from a friend that the wicked imposter had been seen leaving Northampton on foot along the Weedon road and quickly reported the circumstances to Police Sergeant Hector Macleod. Realising that the criminal was too far ahead of him to make any headway on foot, the astute Sergeant called on a local car owner, Jack Harrison, for assistance. He gladly allowed the Sergeant to ride alongside him in his new Benz. Phillips was detained close to the village of Flore and returned to Angel Lane police station, Northampton where he was eventually brought before the quarter sessions in June the same year. Phillips initially protested his innocence, but due to the overwhelming evidence against him changed his plea to guilty to obtaining one shilling by false pretences from the Far Cotton shopkeeper. The other offences were taken into consideration. He was consequently bound over for twelve months to the sum of £10 into the custody of his father. This is the first recorded arrest and chase of a criminal by car by any police force in the United Kingdom and possibly the world.

Chief Constable McCallum was replaced in 1931 by Angus

Arthur Ferguson, a detective constable with the Edinburgh police with an excellent pedigree who inspired during his ten years in office. He was replaced in 1941 by Robert Henry Dundas Bolton who also came of an outstanding pedigree with employment in the Metropolitan Police. Bolton was a greatly respected officer who did much to enhance the image of the force.

These were the senior officers who were in command of the force during the various crimes recorded within this book. They can be classed as either fortunate or unfortunate for being in control of the force when the various murders took place. Each one stood by his officers, whether successful or not during the particular investigations, when often sensational pressures were brought upon various officers by the public and media alike who expected the Chief Constable to sack detectives or officers who failed to apprehend murderers within an inordinately short period of time. The pressures of everyday policing are and have always been difficult to bear. One minute a quiet tranquil beat, the next minute a murder scene, visited, examined and scrutinised by literally hundreds of people. The initial actions of the officer on the scene are critical; one error and the investigation can be ruined – a point which is quickly seized by the press.

The cases recorded within this book are as factually accurate as is possible, the actions of the officers concerned are also faithfully defined and if often these do not seem logical, remember they are the actions of men under pressure and, in the early days of policing with little practical or physical experience or training, just how many could bear the responsibility which these individuals were forced to bear?

# THE
# TROUBLES
# OF A. A. ROUSE

THE straggling village of Hardingstone is situated just a couple of miles to the south-east of Northampton town centre. It is one of those villages which nearly everyone has heard of yet cannot provide a reasonable explanation as to why. Situated off the Nene Way bypass, thousands of motorists drive past the western access to the village every day.

Hardingstone Lane is now an access road onto a huge, eight-junction roundabout, but in 1930 it was a narrow country lane which led directly from Hardingstone village and onto the A508 London Road into Northampton. Much of the lane was destroyed when the new bypass was constructed some years ago but part of it does still exist on either side of the Nene Way. This is easily located as the old lane exited onto the London Road close to where the Eleanor Cross (an edifice erected by Edward I as a memorial to his wife) stands. The other end of what was Hardingstone Lane remains within the village, and entry down what is now almost a narrow, overgrown dirt track is restricted by virtue of a five bar gate having been erected by the landowner. Nothing remains to be seen to indicate that one of the most infamous murder cases ever to occur in Britain took place in this lane.

The burnt out Morris Minor saloon where the grisly remains of the murder victim were found.

At around two o'clock on the morning of 6th November 1930, William Bailey and Alfred Thomas Brown were returning to their Hardingstone homes having attended a bonfire night dance at the Salon in Northampton. It had been a beautiful clear evening and the night air was still filled with the dry aroma of wood smoke from the numerous bonfires which had been torched throughout the previous evening. Turning off the London Road and into Hardingstone Lane the two young men saw in the distance the familiar amber glow of a burning fire. Neither thought too much of the glow, perhaps believing it to be a fire which had not yet burnt itself out. Suddenly, without any warning, a stranger stepped out of a hedge on the south side of the lane close to the young men. The man was wearing a raincoat and carrying a small overnight bag. He looked rather confused and stepped onto the road, walking towards London Road.

Alfred Brown and William Bailey were surprised to see such a respectable looking man stepping out of a hedgerow at that time of night but did not comment on the matter immediately. Instead the two asked each other what the fire ahead could be, when suddenly the stranger intervened and commented in response to their query, 'I think someone has had a bonfire'. Upon this he continued to walk away from the mystified men, who turned to watch him. Upon reaching London Road the stranger at first turned right and walked a couple of steps before turning around and standing aimlessly in the middle of the highway and peering down Hardingstone Lane.

Somewhat perturbed by the man's actions both young men trotted off along the lane towards the apparent blaze. As they turned a slight bend both saw that it was actually a car which was ablaze. Flames crackled and hissed some 20 ft into the air, there was a nauseating smell of burning oil and some other obnoxious odour was evident. The car, a Morris Minor 'Baby' saloon, was engulfed in flame, thus making it physically impossible to approach. The two crossed to the opposite side of the lane in order to pass the vehicle, which gave off such an intense heat that the body was almost melted from the chassis.

Leaving the car behind them, Brown and Bailey ran into the village for assistance. Alfred Brown ran to fetch Bert Copping, the village constable, while William Bailey went for his father, who was the local parish constable. En route a number of village folk were alerted and attended the scene. Though shocked, they sensibly formed a human chain passing buckets of water from a nearby house until eventually, some twelve minutes later, the fire had been extinguished. Steam filled the air and the bent and buckled wreck hissed, cracked and snapped as though in its final moments of painful and tortuous death. The villagers were exhausted and still somewhat bemused by the blaze. Bert Copping took control of the situation and stepped up to the smouldering wreck, peering into what was once its leather clad interior. The policeman noticed what appeared to be a charred black rugby ball lying upon what was once the front driver's seat. Initially Copping thought little of this, until he realised that the object was in fact the horrific remains of a burnt human head.

Alfred Brown shone his torch into the car and the group gasped in horror, for there, laid across both front seats, were the remains of a horribly disfigured human being. Bert Copping noted that the head was lying face down and that the left arm was tucked beneath the torso. The right arm had been burnt off at the elbow. Curiously, the left leg was doubled beneath the torso, whereas so little remained of the right leg that it was difficult to make any judgement upon. Hedley Bailey was ordered to run back to the village and to inform Northampton police headquarters.

Inspector James Lawrence arrived on the scene at approximately three o'clock that same morning and spoke with Bert Copping. The men initially felt that the incident appeared to be accidental death. The body was removed from the car wrapped in sacking and taken to the garage of the Crown Inn, Hardingstone. It was later transferred to Northampton General Hospital where it was placed into a tank of preservative, and looked at occasionally for examination purposes. The vehicle was removed from its position on the road and placed onto the grass verge. A check of its registered owner was made with Scotland Yard by virtue of a rear metal number plate still being intact and bearing the licence plate number MU 1468. Bert Copping informed Inspector Lawrence of the stranger William Bailey and Alfred Brown had met with shortly prior to their discovering the blaze, and a full description of the individual was recorded.

With the obstruction gone from the road and the body safely secured in the garage of the Crown Inn, the police retreated to their various offices until the following morning. Unfortunately, enterprising persons jumped onto the bandwagon, and at around eight o'clock that same morning a freelance photographer by the name of Arthur Ashford popped along to the scene of the fire and

Northampton assizes, where A.A. Rouse was tried.

took several shots of the burnt out wreck. There was nothing wrong with this in itself, but Mr Ashford moved one or two objects around and within the vehicle in order to get shots into perspective, and as the police had failed to organise any photographs at that stage the crime scene had now been interfered with, thus making forensic examination that little bit more difficult.

Inspector Lawrence returned to Hardingstone later that afternoon and was met with the result of his vehicle ownership enquiry. The vehicle belonged to Alfred Arthur Rouse, a commercial traveller for a Leicester firm which manufactured garters and suspenders. Rouse lived in Buxted Road, Friern Barnet, North London. He had last been seen alive by his wife Lillian at around eight o'clock on the night of 5th November when he left their home en route to Leicester on business. The inspector was pleased with the way investigations were proceeding. No problems had been encountered at that stage; that is until around eight o'clock that same evening when a bombshell was dropped upon the unfortunate Inspector. The routine police enquiries were not as routine as he first envisaged, for the body in the car had been deliberately burnt. It was murder!

Suddenly the basic errors of policing took on greater significance; no photographs, no protection of the scene resulting in lost evidence; how Inspector Lawrence must have wished he had not attended the scene. Samples of petrol soaked clothing were found in a crease in the crotch area of the victim's trousers, which at that stage could not positively be identified as being male or female. The logical assumption was that it was the remains of Alfred Arthur Rouse, but just who would wish to kill him and for what purposes? In a press release made by Northamptonshire Police, requests were made for the 'City Gent' seen stepping out of the hedge in Hardingstone Lane by Brown and Bailey to come forward to assist with police enquiries.

Unbeknown to the police at that time, Rouse had actually been the individual sighted by the two witnesses. At two o'clock that fateful morning he had hitched a ride to South Wales in the cab of a lorry. He had eventually arrived in Cardiff and caught a bus to the Welsh pit village of Penybryn. Rouse had gone to visit Ivy Jenkins, a woman whom he had bigamously married in June 1930. Ivy was heavily pregnant and Rouse had told her family that he had purchased a house in Kingston for them; this was a typical Rouse fabrication. Rouse arrived at his wife's home close to eight o'clock in the evening on 6th November. He told the family that it had taken him 18 hours to travel the distance from Northampton, where his car had been stolen. The family offered some sympathy and fed Rouse a hearty supper which was disturbed by an inquisitive neighbour who had purchased a copy of a local newspaper containing a photograph of a burnt out car in Northants in which a human body had been discovered! Rouse must have almost choked upon his meal, yet resolutely he stated, 'That is not my car'.

The following morning Rouse was met with a copy of the *Daily Sketch* which not only bore a photograph of the burnt out car but also mentioned Rouse by name. In an attempt to display his innocence, Rouse stated that he was going to return to London at once in order to have the matter resolved once and for all – after all he had done nothing wrong! A neighbour, Mr Brownhill, who was a local car salesman in Cardiff agreed to run Rouse back to the city in order that he should catch a coach back to London. During this trip he became suspicious of Rouse through some unusual comments he made about the mystery in Northampton-shire. Having dropped Rouse at the coach station and seen him catch the Hammersmith-bound coach, Mr Brownhill dropped into a Cardiff police station and informed them of his suspicions.

As the coach pulled into Hammersmith Broadway coach station detectives arrived on the scene and waited for Alfred Arthur Rouse to alight. One approached him, asked him if he was Mr Rouse and duly detained him. Rouse, obviously agitated, said, 'I am glad it's all over. I was going to Scotland Yard. I'm responsible.' Just what was Rouse responsible for?

Rouse was taken to Hammersmith police station and subse-quently interviewed by detectives who recorded written statements volunteered by him. Rouse frequently altered these statements as his mood changed. The police were quietly amazed at just how much Rouse talked. Granted much of it was nervous banter caused by his present predicament, but it seemed clear to these professional interrogators that Rouse would talk himself into trouble with his nervous chatter.

The following morning he was transferred to Angel Lane police station in Northampton where for the first time he met with Inspector Lawrence, who was curious to know what sort of person Rouse was and just what made him tick. The Inspector had some mundane paperwork to complete that morning but agreed to speak with Rouse in his office. To his surprise the Inspector found Rouse to be quite an affable person, though the suspect's high pitched voice did not exactly meet with his approval. As the Inspector sat at his desk, ostensibly studying the documents to which he was putting his signature, Alfred Arthur Rouse paced up and down the office talking of his past and present lifestyles and providing information which was to be invaluable to investigating police officers and would later prove critical at his trial. Rouse seemed oblivious to the fact that Lawrence was writing down verbatim what he was saying.

The suspect explained to the Inspector that he was a womaniser and that he was on friendly terms with several women but found it to be an expensive game. His final quote was to irrevocably destroy him, 'My harem takes me to several places, and I'm not at home a great deal.' Was this another of Rouse's fairy tales or could it be taken seriously? Investigations commenced into Rouse's background and slowly a picture began to form of the man currently being held on a murder charge. Certainly there was irrefutable evidence that Rouse had had at least 80 plus illicit relationships with women and at least ten of these women had borne him children, many of which he was still secretly providing financial support for. His wife Lillian had no knowledge of his affairs or relationships and deemed him to be a happily married man!

Slowly the police file on Rouse was expanding until there was very little they did not know about him. Born in April 1894 of Irish descent, Rouse enlisted in the 24th Queen's Territorial Regiment. On 29th November 1914 he had married (legally) Lily May Watkings at St. Albans. The following year on 15th March he was sent to fight in France and on the 25th day of the same month received severe wounds to the head and leg. Eventually he was pensioned out of the services in 1916 and from there had commenced his adventures in commercial sales.

Shortly after his release from the services Rouse met with an attractive 14 year old Scots girl, Helen Campbell, whom he duly made pregnant; unfortunately the child died shortly after birth. Rouse contacted a friend who was able to employ the young girl as a house servant, thus ensuring that he could visit her as he saw fit. It seems probable that Rouse did have some feeling for this girl and some two years later he again made her pregnant. Helen insisted that they be married (she wrongly believed Rouse to be divorced from his wife). Rouse agreed and a bogus ceremony was carried out. The couple rented a flat in Islington and Rouse advised both Helen and his real wife that he was to be away from home a lot of the time. He was able in effect to live two separate lives. As always Rouse fell foul of his untruths and Helen realised that he was seeing another woman. He confessed all and even told his real wife of his affair with Helen. Lillian was very understanding and met with Helen Campbell. Both women agreed it would be better for the young child, Arthur, if he were brought up in a home which could provide for him, and Lillian took in the child.

Apart from Helen Campbell, there had been Nellie Tucker whom he had met in 1925. She also had two children to Rouse, the second of which was born in the maternity hospital in City Road, London on 29th October 1930. Nellie Tucker told investigating police officers that Rouse had visited her around seven o'clock on Bonfire Night 1930. He seemed very nervous and agitated. He told her that he was concerned about his mounting debts and that he did not know which way he should turn next. He stayed about one hour before kissing Tucker and telling her he had an appointment and had to drive North! When one includes Ivy Jenkins of Penybryn in this scenario then it is simple to see just why Rouse was a worried man.

The police, were remarkably thorough with their investigations and indeed had their suspect locked up within 36 hours of the crime occurring. Rouse's insurance companies were contacted and it was soon confirmed that Rouse had increased the policy held on his motor vehicle for over £1,000 payable upon death in the car!

The police had a complete case apart from the identity of the victim, but as yet Rouse had not been interviewed to this purpose. Certainly it seemed that Rouse had killed the man in the car in an attempt to defraud the insurance companies, thus providing him with £1,000 and a new life ahead of him, probably with the dead man's identity!

A committal hearing was held at Northampton 16th December 1930. All of the evidence so far uncovered was offered, including the famous 'Harem' statement. The defence counsel claimed that such evidence would prejudice the prisoner's defence, but the objection was unanimously overruled and thus stood. The defence counsel were quite justified in their claim about prejudicial evidence; after all Rouse was being tried for murder not bigamy, what could his sexual promiscuity have to do with his actions on the night of 5th November 1930 other than to destroy his character? The media was full of the 'Harem' story and the odds were well and truly stacked against Rouse. The 'Harem' evidence was not actually heard in court, but the damage by that time had been done.

So the court drama commenced at the Northampton assizes. The prosecution led by the brilliant Norman Birkett KC called witness after witness who revealed the various exploits of Alfred Rouse. William Bailey identified him as the man seen in Hardingstone Lane. The insurance salesman explained how Rouse had taken out extra insurance on his vehicle. During the trial Rouse's real wife Lillian sat in front of the dock staring resolutely in front of her, displaying remarkable fortitude under the circumstances. Occasionally she would look to her disloyal husband and offer a smile of comfort which Rouse would reciprocate. A local shop in Bridge street offered Lillian part time employment in order to assist her in paying for her husband's defence counsel. Lillian gladly took advantage of the offer but unfortunately, although a genuine offer, the media made a massive publicity campaign out of the incident, causing more grief to Lillian than she deserved.

Over the trial days which followed, the case against the defendant tightened its grip. Eminent pathologist Sir Bernard Spilsbury gave evidence as to injuries to the victim and the strange positioning of the body in the vehicle. The prosecution claimed that Rouse selected his victim to be the same build as himself, probably, they claimed, a tramp or a roadster. On arrival in Hardingstone Lane it was claimed that Rouse had rendered the man unconscious by use of a wooden mallet and doused him with petrol. He had then unscrewed the petrol pipe union in the engine, thus providing a logical explanation to the official authorities for the cause of the blaze. The victim was then bundled into the front seats of the car. All that Rouse needed to do was to add a lighted match! Possibly an accurate account of what had transpired, this then was the case for the prosecution.

The defence vehemently denied the allegations and Rouse took to the witness stand in an attempt to refute the evidence. He spoke of how he had met the stranger (whose name he did not know) in London, at the Tally Ho corner to be precise. The man was going North in search of employment. Together they travelled to Hardingstone where Rouse felt the urge to relieve himself. He asked the stranger to pour some petrol from the spare can in the back seat into the tank in order to ensure their arrival in Leicester. The stranger requested a cigar which Rouse provided prior to relieving himself behind the hedge. He had taken his overnight bag with him as he had noticed the other fellow looking at it and actually touching it. Whilst behind the hedge Rouse claimed to have heard the explosion of the car igniting. He said, 'I ran towards the car which was in flames. I saw the man inside and tried to open the door but could not as the car was a mass of flames . . . I was all of a shake. I did not know what to do and ran as hard as I could along the road where I saw the two men . . . I lost my head and did not know what to do and really don't know what I have done since.' It seemed that Rouse had offered a perfectly reasonable explanation, equally as believable as the prosecution case, yet someone was

# JUDGES DISMISS
## ROUSE'S APPEAL.

---

## Lord Hewart's Tribute to Mr. Justice Talbot's Masterly Summing-Up.

---

## PROSECUTION'S "ERRORS."

IN the Court of Criminal Appeal on Monday the last legal battle for the life of Alfred Arthur Rouse, the 36-year-old commercial traveller who lies under sentence of death for the murder of the unknown man in the blazing car at Hardingstone was waged—and lost! The appeal was dismissed.

Giving judgment, Lord Hewart said that the only ground of the appeal in that court was that there was no case to go to the jury. That submission was made by Rouse's counsel at the conclusion of the case for the Crown in the court below, and Mr. Justice Talbot then held that there were matters which it was proper to lay before a jury.

"With regard to the summing-up, Sir Patrick Hastings has used the word 'unassailable.' It is indeed, if I may say so, a masterly summing-up' and Sir Patrick has been able to find only one part of one expression to which he takes exception. We see no reason why this appeal should be allowed, and it is dismissed."

No judgment was delivered by Justices Avory and Humphreys, and the court immediately rose.

Suave charm and good looks, bigamy and murder – the sensational elements of the case against Rouse caught the public imagination and filled the headlines.

wrong. It was not too long before the defendant's tale began to crumble.

Norman Birkett KC asked Rouse why he felt the need to tell lies to the Jenkins family on his arrival in South Wales, and just why he took almost 48 hours to report the incident to the authorities. Rouse seemed lost for a moment, then commented upon how he had no faith in the smaller localised police stations, indeed had he not been on his way to the very fountainhead of the British police service, Scotland Yard, when he was arrested? The reply failed to impress Birkett, who maintained his unrelenting pressure upon the defendant. His response was to ask why Rouse said he was 'responsible' for the incident in Hardingstone. Faltering, Rouse explained, 'In the police eyes the owner of the car is responsible for anything that happens to that car. Correct me if I am wrong.'

Suddenly Alfred Arthur Rouse began to display an air of arrogance, as though he felt in control of events in the courtroom. When asked about the unfortunate victim of the blaze, Rouse displayed so little emotion towards the dead man that it became clear that he actually saw the victim as little more than a thing, an intangible object with no feelings. Birkett pressed home fact after fact. If the man was supposed to be outside the car pouring petrol then why was he laid across the front seats of the vehicle with the door closed? Rouse could offer no explanation. Next the prosecution put to Rouse that the man was within the car when the fire started. Rouse confirmed this, adding that the doors to the car were both actually closed. 'How then', enquired Birkett, 'was a burnt off right foot found lying outside the vehicle?' Rouse visibly began to wilt, his willpower and concentration had been broken.

Birkett turned to the court and stated that it was his opinion that Rouse had knocked the victim unconscious with a wooden mallet (found near the car) with a view to having the authorities believe that the charred remains were Alfred Arthur Rouse. The prisoner rocked in the dock and denied the allegations but had no ammunition left to defend himself with. Birkett quite clearly won the day.

At the end of the six day trial the jury took just one hour and 15 minutes to reach a verdict of Guilty of murder. The judge assumed the 'Black Cap' and, looking Rouse sternly in the eyes, said, 'You have been found guilty of this crime for which the law appoints one sentence, and only one, and it is that which I now pronounce upon you – that you be taken from hence to the place of lawful execution, and be hanged by the neck until you are dead and that your body be afterwards buried in the precincts of that prison in which you were last confined, and may God have mercy upon your soul.' Alfred Arthur Rouse stood stern faced in the dock and accepted his fate with apparent fortitude. As he was led away he looked to his wife Lillian, who stared blankly at him before attempting to lift her hand in the gesture of a wave. The moment was lost amongst the tears of the numerous weeping females within the courtroom, some of whom could not have heard of Rouse until the case hit the headlines but had since fallen for his suave charm and devilish good looks.

So, at eight o'clock on the morning of Tuesday 10th March 1931 at Bedford prison, Alfred Arthur Rouse was hanged. He had to be led from the condemned cell to the gallows and became very distressed at the thought of his eternal fate. His final words were saved for his wife Lillian, 'Goodbye dear, you are the best woman I have ever known. I hope the future will hold greater happiness for you.' If only Rouse had displayed such loyalty to his wife whilst he was alive surely he would never have got himself into the situation which led to an unfortunate man's death and ultimately his own.

The identity of the dead man was never confirmed; this was the one secret Rouse took to his grave with him. Having researched this crime for many years and scrutinised every document which exists on the case I have come to my own conclusions as to the identity of the unknown man. A William Edwards from the

Derbyshire area seems to be the most likely candidate. Edwards was known to have travelled to London around mid 1930 in search of employment. He had previously been employed in the Derbyshire pits and sought fame and fortune from the bright lights of the city, which was never forthcoming, though he is now possibly the most famous anonymous murder victim of all time! The mystery, unfortunately, must remain, as it is impossible to prove that the man in question was Edwards. The unknown man was given a full Christian burial in Hardingstone village; what is more curious is the fact that buried at the foot of an oak cross which stands above the grave, is a metal case containing certain papers appertaining to the case and a true record of how the man died. To this day the cross stands and bears the simple inscription; 'In memory of an unknown man. Died Nov 6 1930'. The grave is to the rear of Hardingstone village church.

# THE
# EAST HADDON MYSTERY

IN July 1892 a murder took place where the body was not discovered for a full 16 days after the event. The crime was horrific and to this day a certain amount of mystery is still connected with it. The East Haddon mystery is perhaps one of the most intriguing murder stories anyone could ever read, it is certainly one of the county's most incredible murder cases.

The picturesque village of East Haddon is situated along the Northampton to Rugby road. It has a history dating back to the Domesday Book where it is recorded as 'Eddone'. Since those times the village and community has prospered. By 1892 it was served with a railway connection which boosted the population of the village to around the 650 mark, the majority of whom were farming people. Village life in the late 19th century was very peaceful and content and the community tended to be self supportive; certainly in the main everyone knew their neighbour.

August Bank Holiday weekend 1892 was one of the hottest on official record. The heat ensured that most people relaxed over the holiday period, and for Charles Hadley, a young local man, Saturday 6th August was just another day in normal country life. The burning summer sun made the fresh country aromas more pungent than normal. Charles Hadley came across a particularly foul stench, emanating from an old sack in the bottom of a six ft ditch on the turnpike road about half a mile from Althorp Park railway station, on the road to East Haddon and Long Buckby. Hadley initially thought the smell was that of a dead sheep or other farm animal which had died and lay putrefying in the ditch and was curious as to why the dead animal should be wrapped inside a sack. Taking a stick he prodded and poked at the package at the bottom of the ditch and managed to split the outer wrapping, revealing a white mass of skin which was in an advanced stage of decomposition. The stench from the bundle was unbearable. As Hadley gasped for clean air he managed to fight off the urge to vomit and decided to leave his morbid find for the time being and to inform someone about it.

At the village public house Hadley soon advised many of the regulars of his find and explained how it was wrapped in sacking.

The Red Lion public house in East Haddon, where in 1892, the final remains of Annie Pritchard were taken and where the inquest took place.

The villagers listened to the tale and decided to investigate matters and so half a dozen or so menfolk walked to the ditch to view and examine the bundle and its contents. John Chapman volunteered to climb down into the ditch and to open the bundle. Country folk were not afraid of touching or being near a dead animal, after all it was more or less an everyday occurrence. But neither Chapman nor the others had bargained for what they were about to witness, for as the bundle was split open by the inquisitive villager a rotting pair of human legs literally flopped out of the wrapping. The flesh was dropping from the bones and it was clear that the remains were those of a partially clothed female who was still wearing a bloodstained dress.

The body was removed from the ditch and taken to the Red Lion public house in East Haddon upon a pallet. The remains were examined by Doctor Churchhouse, a local surgeon, who confirmed that the body was indeed that of a young woman minus head and arms. The woman had been dead upwards of three weeks to a month. The impossible had occurred in the very midst of this tiny community; murder!

The Borough and the County Police were both informed of the grisly find but they had little information to act upon. The press revealed that the material of the dress worn by the victim was of a good quality, therefore the inference was that the woman must have originated from a respectable background. The remains had been originally enfolded in a sugar bag then wrapped in a coarse hessian type material. One corner of the sugar bag bore a white label on which the words 'E.M.RAE. Northampton, L.& N.W.' were printed.

An inquest into the shocking discovery opened at the Red Lion public house on Tuesday 8th August 1892. The investigating authorities were at a total loss. Edward MacRae, whose name had been found upon the label on the sugar bag, was called to give evidence as to why human remains should be wrapped in one of his sugar bags. This was easily explained by MacRae, who advised

Annie Pritchard with her lover and murderer, Andrew George MacRae.

the authorities that he was a bacon factor, having a stall on the Northampton market and a warehouse in Dychurch Lane. The wrappings in which the body was found were regularly sold to numerous persons all over the county. With this in mind the label was rejected as being of any evidential value or bearing on the murder. The inquest was adjourned for a further month to allow the investigating authorities time to look into the matter, but one month later little was resolved and so a verdict of 'Found Dead' was returned, which generally left matters unresolved. Every effort was made to identify the remains, articles were featured in the pages of the local press and at one stage it did appear that the remains were those of a Miss Tite who had been missing from her

Northampton home for some considerable time. The clothing in which the remains were dressed was identified by Mrs Tite as being similar to that worn by her daughter on the day she left home. However, Miss Tite returned home to her mother shortly after the story had been printed in a local newspaper.

It seemed that the investigation was slowly being run down as the authorities failed to provide any answers as to who, why and where. It was the dogged curiosity of a local journalist who refused to let the matter slip from memory which eventually presented the authorities with a major breakthrough in the case. A copy of the label found in the sugar bag was reproduced and printed in the local press. This in turn jolted the memory of a Mrs Bland, a dealer in secondhand clothes who resided in College Street, Northampton. Bland contacted the police and advised them that Andrew George MacRae, brother of Edward MacRae, bacon factor, had sold her a quantity of women's and babies' linen in the latter part of July 1892. She had found this strange as MacRae had only recently become a father. Andrew George MacRae was requested to attend Angel Lane police station in Northampton as soon as possible, but took his time in responding to the police request. Eventually he was brought to the station on the direct instruction of Superintendent Alexander.

MacRae was 36 years of age and at that time was working for his brother Edward as an assistant at the market stall. He also had a set of keys to the Dychurch Lane warehouse where he held certain responsibilities. Married with two young children, he was currently lodging in St John Street in the town; his wife and family were still residing in Birmingham. MacRae was asked why he was in possession of women's and babies' linen and why he had sold them. In reply to this he blatantly lied, informing the police that his wife had sent him them to sell in order to raise money. Unknown to MacRae his wife Harriet was contacted and denied the claims made by her husband, stating that she knew nothing of any linen.

Andrew George MacRae was arrested on the morning of Saturday 3rd September. He was formally charged with the murder of an unknown woman, a claim which he vehemently denied. He was brought before the county magistrates on Monday 5th September and remanded until Saturday 10th September 1892. During this time the police were actively involved in enquiries in Birmingham and soon learned that a woman by the name of Annie Pritchard had left her Birmingham home in the previous March and had not been seen nor heard of since. The Pritchard family, it transpired, resided close to the home of Andrew MacRae and the two were well known to each other! Indeed an intimate relationship between Annie and Andrew had been evident for some considerable time.

Annie Pritchard was 32 years of age and had told her friends and family that she had been courting a lithographic artist by the name of Guy Anderson for some time. Anderson, she claimed, had asked her to travel to Liverpool to marry her and then to emigrate with him to America. None of the family had ever seen or spoken with Anderson, but they felt sure that Annie would not lie about such a thing and did not prevent her from leaving. Fortunately, for Annie, as she was travelling to Northampton to be with her true lover Andrew MacRae, she met with a man who told her he was going to Liverpool on a visit. Hastily Annie scribbled a letter to her parents explaining that she was now married and would have left the country with Guy by the time they read the letter. She then persuaded the stranger to post this letter upon his arrival in Liverpool, which he did and so the Pritchard family believed their daughter to be making a new life for herself in America. Just two people knew the truth of the situation and those were the two lovers themselves.

Carelessly, MacRae and Pritchard took lodgings in St John Street under the name of Mr and Mrs Anderson, a factor which was to prove damning at the later court hearing. On the 23rd June 1892 Annie had given birth to an illegitimate child of the relationship with MacRae, and now the child's disappearance was as great a mystery as that of the disappearance of Annie Pritchard.

Police enquiries were astute and successful. A Mrs Elliott came forward, volunteering the information that on the 20th July 1892 she had met with Mr and Mrs Anderson and child in St John Street. The family were moving lodgings to Derby Road. Mrs Elliott had carried the baby part of the way as far as Bridge Street, where they had parted as Mr Anderson had stated that he had to go to the post office. This was the last sighting of mother and child alive. It was alleged by police that MacRae had left Mrs Elliott and taken Annie and the child to the bacon warehouse in Dychurch Lane and had there murdered them. Other circumstantial evidence came to the fore when it was revealed that MacRae had twice hired a dog cart on the 26th July; this was the mode of transport used to deposit the remains in the ditch.

Scene of the murder at Dychurch Lane; the MacRae bacon warehouse once stood where the scaffolding is erected.

The Dychurch Lane warehouse was systematically searched under the direct supervision of Superintendent Alexander. Approximately 30 pieces of calcined bone were found and removed. Some bore score marks which had evidently been made by the shark-style teeth of a saw. A surgeon later confirmed these bones to be part of a hand and some of an upper arm. In the copper were traces of brown human hair which matched the colour of Annie's hair. Nothing was discovered of the baby.

The trial of Andrew MacRae commenced at Northampton on the 17th November. To the amazement and anger of the public MacRae was charged with the singular murder of Annie Pritchard, nothing was said of the slaughter of an innocent and defenceless child. This undoubtedly turned public opinion against MacRae who seemed amused by all the commotion surrounding his trial.

Mr Justice Kennedy opened the trial by swearing in the jury and carrying out official court commitments. With this complete he adjourned the trial for lunch. During this adjournment a most extraordinary incident occurred which had never before taken place in an English court of law. A police officer was being sworn in as a bailiff to take charge of the jury during the retirement for lunch. While this was occurring one juror, James Asplin, left the courthouse in order to return to his lodgings to fetch an important letter which he had to post. Asplin's absence was noticed and a constable was sent to search for the missing juror, who was located in the street some 25 minutes later. Counsel were invited to speak with Justice Kennedy on the matter, but no decision could be made and so the judge advised the jury that they must remain together under police supervision that evening whilst he sought guidance from elsewhere. The following morning the unfortunate Mr Asplin was fined £50 for gross contempt of court and severely admonished for his actions.

Some 47 witnesses were called over the days which followed, each one adding weight to the considerable evidence already against MacRae. In his defence MacRae attempted to explain that the father of the missing child had in fact been Guy Anderson and that Annie had left him some time ago in order to marry Anderson and to emigrate to America. The authorities were able to disprove this fabrication. There had been someone by the name of G. Anderson residing in Birmingham some 18 months prior, but there was no evidence of him being an artist nor leaving these shores. Andrew MacRae's defence was ripped to shreds by an accurate prosecution case. No one ever really believed in his innocence but certainly any doubts which had remained were successfully removed by the evidence against him.

It was Christmas Eve when the jury retired from the courtroom to consider their verdict. They took just one and a half hours to find MacRae guilty of murdering Annie Pritchard. Crowds outside the court cheered enthusiastically when the verdict reached them. Mr Justice Kennedy asked MacRae if he knew of any reason why judgement should not be passed upon him. MacRae turned to the jury and said, 'Any sentence that might be passed upon me gives me no terror because I am innocent of the charge.' Further to this he said that the witness testimonies against him were abominable lies. Finally, in an emotive last gesture, he calmly stated 'Each and every one of you this day have become what you have made me – a murderer, you have widowed a good devoted wife and made fatherless loving children. Go to your homes with clear consciences if you can, for as long as you live your consciences will accuse you!' The sentence of death was then passed upon MacRae who displayed no emotion whatsoever at the thought of his fate. It seems that his closing speech evoked some sympathy towards him, as rumours were rife a short time after his execution that the police were still actively engaged in enquiries into Annie Pritchard's murder, but there is no official record of any such enquiries having been made.

Andrew MacRae was hanged at Northampton gaol on the morning of Tuesday 10th January 1893. The executioner, James Billington, was paid the sum of ten pounds for carrying out the gruesome task which was performed with some ease. MacRae made no final confession nor did he utter any remorse for his sins. His body was buried within the prison grounds, where it remained until 1931 when the gaol was demolished, and along with numerous others his remains were dug up after midnight and transported via a refuse cart to a common grave at Towcester cemetery, where they still lie.

The remains of Annie Pritchard were interred in the new cemetery at East Haddon; it was the first burial in that graveyard with the grave being situated along its boundary. The funeral was well attended and shortly afterwards a memorial stone was erected above the grave, paid for by local contributions and bearing the inscription, 'I was a stranger and you took me in.' This was in reference to the fact that each of the local parishes had declined to allow a murdered body to be buried within their parish graveyards and it was only the insistence of the Reverend Ruston, Congregational Minister for Long Buckby which eventually forced East Haddon to take the remains, though it was officially under their jurisdiction anyway. The grave is still clearly marked to this day and stands alone close to an entrance gate.

# KEEP IT IN THE FAMILY

RELATED killers are rare, especially so when the crimes committed are separated by two decades. Yet Northamptonshire can boast such a scenario during the 18th century. Both were women and both were the worst kind of killer, the poisoner. Neither woman had any direct knowledge of the other and the pair most certainly had never met.

The history of this case begins in the year 1715 when Elizabeth Miller, as she was then known, met Richard Treslar. The Treslar family were quite affluent, unlike the Millers who, although good people, had the misfortune to have a daughter who used her feminine wiles to her best advantage. She had always been a scheming and cunning girl, a trait which her family hoped would cure itself as she matured. Unfortunately this was not to be the case.

It came as some surprise to the village of Badby, which is situated to the west of Northampton, when Elizabeth was seen to be in the company of Richard Treslar, who was locally accepted as being a 'fine young man'. It seems that Richard became enamoured of Elizabeth and the couple married after a very short courtship. The marriage caused much consternation to the Treslar family, who believed Elizabeth to be marrying their son for his wealth. Despite their secret pleas to Richard, the marriage went ahead and the couple came to reside in a pleasant cottage close to the village church. The Treslar family opted to withhold much of Richard's inheritance until they were sure of his new wife's objectives. Yet the worries seemed misplaced, as Elizabeth was apparently a loyal and trustworthy wife to Richard, caring for his every need, though she must have noticed the animosity the Treslar family felt towards her. Despite these problems the marriage seemed to be a success and over the weeks which followed Elizabeth became more and more accepted as part of the family.

Richard Treslar's personal principles did not allow him to partake of ale nor to eat too much meat, his favoured refreshment being the sweet taste of sugar mixed with a few drops of fresh water taken from nearby streams. Richard would walk through the countryside for hours on end watching and studying the wildlife in its natural habitat. He enjoyed the peacefulness away from the village and much preferred his own company. Soon, however, Richard had educated Elizabeth to enjoy the countryside and the pair were often seen walking through local fields and woodland.

One beautiful summer afternoon in 1715, the villagers of Badby might have noticed Elizabeth and Richard Treslar out walking in the fields close to the village. With the pair was David Winters, a close friend of Richard. As they approached one of Richard's favourite streams, Elizabeth Treslar dropped a small paper package upon the grass, knowing full well that Richard had seen her do so. Richard bent down and tentatively opened the tiny package, seeing what he assumed to be sugar grains ready to be mixed into his favourite drink. Gleefully he added the grains to a little fresh water and drank the lot. What Richard Treslar had actually consumed was a lethal dosage of white mercury, similar in texture and appearance to sugar.

After a brief stroll the trio returned to the village, with the Treslars returning home. Richard Treslar was in a jocular mood,

The fields close to Badby, so enjoyed by Richard Treslar, where he found the package of mercury dropped by his wife.

possibly caused by the thought of his wife's keenness to please him. After a few hours Richard began to experience severe stomach pains, causing him to writhe and scream in agony. Elizabeth played the part of the perfect caring wife. She quickly sent for the surgeon, as well as notifying the Treslar family of their son's sudden illness. As Treslar passed away Elizabeth sobbed hysterically, apparently inconsolable, arousing great sympathy from family and villagers alike.

Richard's death was diagnosed as death by natural causes. His odd eating and drinking habits were blamed for his painful death and without further delay he was buried in the local churchyard. For a few days after the funeral Elizabeth mourned the death of her husband, but she was soon seen to revert to her old habits and was befriended by a number of local men, a fact which displeased the Treslar family.

Some eight to nine weeks after Richard's funeral, Elizabeth Treslar disappeared. The village and woodland was searched but there was no sign of her. There were tales of her having been eaten by wild animals whilst out walking along her husband's favourite paths, others claimed she had thrown herself into a river and had been carried away in the flowing water. All searches proved negative and the village gossips began to talk of other matters. Suddenly Richard's death began to be seen as somewhat suspicious. Treslar had always been a fit and healthy man up to the time of his marriage. Now that Elizabeth had disappeared from the area, it seemed logical to think that she might have left of her own free will before suspicions were cast against her. Suddenly this peaceful hamlet was excitedly buzzing with the talk of murder.

The Treslar family normally remained aloof to local gossip but certain members of the community made it their business to advise the family of local doubts and opinions. Two years passed by and the incident was all but forgotten in the local community. Only Richard Treslar's sister found it difficult to forget her brother's death and vowed to avenge him.

Then, during a social visit to England's capital city, she accidentally met with Elizabeth Treslar. At first she was unsure that it was the woman she had been searching for, so to be sure she called out her name. Elizabeth Treslar responded to the call and suddenly realised that she was confronted with her dark past. Frantically, Elizabeth attempted to flee but was caught by her pursuer, who once again asked her name and accused her of murder. Elizabeth attempted to deny any knowledge of the Treslar family but was unable to convince her captor.

Both women returned to Northampton and en route Elizabeth confessed her crime and spoke of her deep remorse and how she had failed to sleep peacefully since the event. On arrival in

Northampton, Elizabeth was handed over to the authorities, who questioned her for a number of hours before she finally confessed all.

After a brief trial at Northampton she was found guilty of murder and sentenced to death by hanging. At the execution, which took place on Northampton Heath (along the Kettering Road), crowds gathered and screamed in jubilation as she was dragged beneath the gallows on an open backed cart. Without warning Elizabeth, who had seemed depressed, began to act like a woman possessed. She screamed obscenities at the spectators, causing those who witnessed the event to claim she was possessed by a malevolent and evil spirit! The noose was placed around her neck and the cart drawn from beneath her feet. Elizabeth struggled to remain conscious and visibly danced her way to death for

The village church at Badby where, despite the protestations of his family, Richard Treslar married Elizabeth Miller. He was to be buried there within the year.

almost 15 minutes before losing her desperate fight with the grim reaper.

Little could anyone have realised that a direct relation of Elizabeth on her mother's side, another Elizabeth, would be condemned to death and burnt at the stake (within a few yards of where Mrs Treslar had been dispatched) some 20 years later!

Elizabeth Fawson was the daughter of a Mr Bull, a butcher in the tiny village of Helmdon to the south-west of Towcester. Elizabeth Fawson had been brought up in a tolerant and kind manner according to the family's circumstances and no child could have expected more from their parents. At first she had been a willing and keen student, hoping to make something of her life. She could read and write at an early age and was provided with every opportunity to improve herself academically. Part of the maturing process included her being placed in certain affluent houses outside the county boundaries where she could be taught the ways of the gentry and general housemaid's responsibilities. During this period her character appeared to change, she suddenly became belligerent and sought male companionship as often as possible. She often found herself in trouble with her masters, resulting in her rapid return to Helmdon.

The villagers of Helmdon were surprised on her return to find that she had become rude and impolite. Her father attempted as best he could to rectify matters, but Elizabeth was too strong willed and disobedient to heed any warnings. Soon she was keeping company with the more unsavoury characters of the area, including one Edward Monks who was a local rogue and vagabond. The relationship between this pair seemed quite strong and for a long while they were inseparable.

To everyone's surprise, Elizabeth announced her impending marriage to Thomas Fawson, who was the son of local gentry. Thomas's friends attempted to dissuade him from the relationship but found him stubborn in his decision; he seemed totally oblivious to the type of woman he was to marry. On Sunday 18th May

1735, the couple married and it was quite obvious from the outset that Elizabeth felt little emotion or desire for her new husband. For her it was a marriage of pure convenience. Thomas Fawson was virtually left alone at his home whilst the new wife gallivanted around the area with Edward Monks, yet still he seemed to know nothing of these meetings. Thomas took to working the land and regularly assisted his own employees in reaping the harvest. He did everything within his power to endear himself to his wife but all his approaches were rejected.

Thomas often returned home from a day's work in the meadows to sit down to a meal of bread and ale, which would have been prepared by Elizabeth. After just 38 days of marriage, Elizabeth Fawson added sixpenn'orth of white mercury to the bread which was consumed by her hungry husband. Later that same evening Thomas fell ill with stomach cramp. A doctor was summoned and astutely recognised the symptoms of poisoning. Wisely, he avoided divulging his suspicions to Elizabeth but instead told her that her husband had a virus and was beyond medical treatment. As death drew close Thomas began to vomit blood and was out of his mind with agonising pain. Eventually he passed away after suffering the searing pains related to poisoning.

Calmly the doctor left the Fawson household, instructing Elizabeth that he would return later in order to remove the body. In fact, he at once travelled to Northampton, where he reported his beliefs to the authorities. Elizabeth Fawson was arrested and brought to trial for the murder of her husband. The subsequent trial was a straightforward affair and took place on Thursday 17th July 1735 at Northampton. There was little problem in proving her guilt and she was sentenced to death by being burnt at the stake! She was to be detained in Northampton gaol until the date of execution which was set for August 8th. During this time Elizabeth, who was normally an extrovert, became a virtual recluse. She refused to talk with anyone and would not look into the faces of fellow prisoners.

# A True and Faithful ACCOUNT of the Last CONFE[illegible]ION

On the Day of Execution (as deliver'd to a Divine who attended her) of *Eliz. Fawson*, who was, on the 8th Day of *August*, [illegible]35, burnt to Ashes for poysoning her Husband, *Thomas Fawson*, jun. of *Weston* and *Weedon*, in the County of *Northampton*, on *Wednesday* the 18th of *June* last.

As also a True Account of the Burning of *Eliz. Treslar*, of *Badby* in the said County (a R[illegible] of the said *Eliz. Fawson*) in the Y[illegible] 1715 on the same Heath, for a Fact of the same Nature.

ELIZABETH FAWSON, late of *Weston* and *Weedon*, near *Towcester*, in the County of *Northampton*, the unhappy Person, subject of the following Discourse, was Daughter of one *Bull*, a Butcher, at the *Red-Lyon* at *Helmdon*, in the said County of *Northampton*, and was born, as is reported, on or about the Day of the Execution and Burning of *Elizabeth Treslar*, of *Badby*, in the said County, (who is said to be a very near Relation, by the Mother's Side, to the above-named *Elizabeth Fawson*) and was condemn'd, executed and burned at the Summer Assizes in 1715, for a Fact of the same Nature, viz. *For Poisoning her Husband, Richard Treslar*; which was done in the following manner, just 11 Weeks after her Marriage:

Being walking in the Fields with her said Husband, and another Person, she purposely and designedly, tho' privately, dropp'd in the Way they were walking a Paper, neatly ty'd up, of White Sugar, in which was mix'd some White Mercury; which Paper so dropp'd her Husband took up, and opening it, and believing it to be Sugar, she had him (it being hot Weather) to a Spring, knowing her Husband frequently drank Sugar and Water, where she took care to mix the said Preparation in some Water he then drank, which soon had its desir'd Effect; But as there was no publick Orat[illegible]on of his being poison'd, he was buried without any noise to do, and she continued some time (about eight or nine Weeks) in the County after her Husband's Burial; but disappearing all on a sudden, and no Person knowing where nor which way she was gone, the Country began to believe, on recollecting the Suddenness of Mr. *Treslar's* Death, and other Circumstances, that he must certainly have been poison'd, and that by his Wife only. However, no one could tell any Tidings of Mrs. *Treslar*, his Wife, or which way she was gone, untill about two Years afterwards, when Mrs. *Treslar*, Sister of the said *Richard Treslar*, was going to *London*, accidentally saw her Sister-in-law, and challenging her by Name, she confidently deny'd herself to be the Person, which confirm'd the other in the Opinion she had of her Brother being poison'd; therefore she did immediately seize her, and being carried before a Justice, she confess'd the Fact, for which, as above-recited, she received Sentence, and was accordingly executed and burn'd within about 100 Yards of the Place on the same Heath where the the said *Elizabeth Fawson* has receiv'd the Reward and Sentence due for such perfidious and unnatural Actions.

But to proceed to the Behaviour and past Life of *Elizabeth Fawson*, the Person we are now discoursing of, as well from her Infancy, as to the Time of her Execution on *Friday* the 8th Day of *August*, 1735. She was brought up by her Parents in a tolerable handsome manner, according to their Circumstances, and learnt to read and write, as well as plain Work, &c. needful for one of her Station; and lived with her Friends till fit for Service, when she was placed out accordingly, in some of which Places she behaved as to give Satisfaction, and especially untill she came acquainted with some young Persons, whose Conversations were the perfect and first Step to her Ruin, but notwithstanding she had for a long Time past lost her Character (the only Comfort for a Person in her Rank) *Tho. Fawson*, the unhappy Person poison'd, who could not but have heard much of her) fell very deeply in Love with her, and although he was but about Seventeen Years of Age, none of his Friends and Relations could prevail with him to desist from her Acquaintance, and was accordingly to his fixed Resolutions on Sunday the 18th of *May*, married. And although it was observed, that there was not much Affection on her side to the said Match, yet [illegible] Hopes of Lucre and Gain set all Things for the present in a seeming quiet Posture, and as the Friends on one side were very fond and desirous of the Match, so were the other as much averse: However as they were married, the Husband's Friends did in a most Christian manner receive their new Daughter-in-Law, and gave all suitable Encouragement to their living a happy and comfortable Life. But such was the unhappy Fate and Disposition of this Woman, that she cou'd not be satisfied in the true Affections of a loving Husband (who had married her purely for Love, without the least Hopes or Sight of farther Views) that she could not refrain from [illegible] immediately means to dispatch him, in order to make Way, as she conceived, for one more endearing to her, which she effected [illegible] *Wednesday*, the 18th of *July*, being five Weeks and three Days after her Marriage, by preparing a Mess of Bread and Beer in which was privately conveyed Six-penny worth of *White Mercury*, which she had that Day bought of an Apothecary in *Brackley*, and when he came from his Labours in the Fields, she in a pretended loving Sort gave him to refresh him after his Day's Work, of which Fact on *Thursday*, the 17th Day of *July* 1735, she was on the most plain Circumstances convicted, and received Sentence, *To be burnt to Death*, as the Law requires in such Cases.

After Condemnation [illegible] and indeed all the Time before, whilst in Prison) she was shy of all sorts of Company, and always avoided looking at any body or letting any one see her Face that spoke or came near her, and could never be brought to answer any Questions that were asked her on Account of her Husband's Death, or any other Affairs. In the Whole she seem'd to be very sullen, and of a harden'd Disposition, and by all the Arguments that could be used by several Divines, who frequently visited her, (and as it is most apparently known, spared no Pains to bring her to a sincere and unfeigned Repentance of her grievous Sins) could not be brought to any publick Confession of that or any other Crimes, (some of which are very hard on her Character, and of the same Nature as that for which she died) all which is and must certainly be look'd on as owing to the Pride of a near Relation, who frequently visited her, and has as frequently been observ'd strictly to enjoin her to no open Confession whatever.

The Day of her Execution being come, she was drawn (attended by many Thousands of Spectators) on a Sledge to the Stake prepared for her a small Distance from the Road leading to *Kettering*, on *Northampton* Heath, but all the way would not suffer her Face to be seen, having a Black Silk Hood quite over it, which she never once suffer'd to be uncover'd) and being asked by a proper Person attending (her Sullenness and continued Silence giving just Room) if she had nothing to say to the Word in relation to her Crime, &c. answer'd, That she had nothing to say, more than what she had revealed to a Reverend Divine, who often attended her after Sentence of Death, and of which the under Letter contains the Particulars, but desired immediately to be dispatch'd out of this World; and after she was lifted out of the Sledge, she privately requested an attending Officer, that she might be quite dead before the Fire was lighted: And being fix'd to the Stake, and the Rope about her Neck for some small time, she desired again to be dispatch'd, and accordingly the Stool was drawn from under her, and the Fire being lighted as directed, in about two or three Hours she was entirely consum'd.

SIR,

*THE Death of the Unhappy Mrs.* Fawson *gives me a Liberty which before I had not of communicating to you some Particulars relating to her, which may contain an Answer to your Enquiries, and which on the whole I did not think necessary to conceal.*

*The second Time I visited her since she was under Sentence of Death she desired to speak with me alone; and then told me, that she could not be satisfied, till she had confess'd to me, as she said she had before done to a worthy Friend of mine, that she was indeed guilty of the Crime for which she was to die. I took the Freedom to ask her whether she were provoked to this unhappy Action by any ill Usage from her Husband? She assured me with great Earnestness, That she was not; and that during the Time of their short Marriage she never received [illegible] Unkindness from him: But that the true Reason was her [illegible] Affection for another Person, who was so far from being Confederate with her in her Attempt on Mr.* Fawson's *Life, that he did not apprehend any thing of the Regard she had for him, and had never seen her since her Marriage. I told her I concluded that during the Interval of Time between her forming and executing this detestable Design, her Mind must be in great Terror and Distress; but, to my Amazement, she declared that it was not, and that she felt very little Discomposure, 'till she saw the Effect of the Poison, and then found herself impress'd with some Sentiments of Compassion rather than of Fear. I then mentioned to her what had been commonly reported concerning her Falshood to her Husband's Bed, and her having been suspected of poisoning a Fellow Servant some time ago; but she solemnly denied both, with repeated Appeals to Heaven as to her Innocence, and seem'd desirous that I would do her publick Justice as to both these Charges if I had an Opportunity.*

*I earnestly press'd her to make an open Confession, but she seem'd utterly averse to it. She appear'd heartily sorry for what she had done, and attended to Religious Instructions and Prayers with great Seriousness and many Tears; but how far her Repentance was Sincere, Genuine, and Evangelical, He only is capable of judging before whom she has now made her Appearance, and from whom she has received her final Sentence.*

On the same Day *Elizabeth Wilkinson* was hanged, who was condemned at the last Assizes at *Northampton* for picking of Pockets.

An 18th century broadsheet detailing the crimes and executions of Elizabeth Treslar and Elizabeth Fawson, poisoners both.

It was not too long before the authorities discovered that while she had been serving as a domestic in a house outside the county, a fellow manservant had died under suspicious circumstances, not dissimilar to those under which her husband had died! Various attempts were made to link the crimes but Elizabeth vehemently denied all such allegations. She continued to maintain her silence about her husband's death.

Finally Friday 8th August arrived. Elizabeth Fawson had still not confessed to her crime; the only person to whom she would speak was a local priest who was sworn to secrecy by the prisoner and maintained a silence about the affair. It was a cool crisp February morning when Elizabeth Fawson was drawn upon a sledge to the specially prepared stake on the Heath. Thousands of spectators were in attendance and the mood of the crowd was unusually subdued. Upon being tied to the stake Elizabeth was again asked by the authorities if she required to confess her guilt. Her reply displayed little emotion. She intimated that she had spoken with the priest and now wished to be dispatched from this earth as efficiently and expediently as was possible. As she was being strapped to the stake she requested to speak with an attending officer, whom she asked to ensure that she was dead before the bracken was lit. The official agreed to see that this was so. Fawson was then garrotted until it was felt she was dead. The bracken was lit and soon engulfed the limp human form secured to the wooden stake. Only those close enough noticed that suddenly Elizabeth Fawson's head jerked back, and saw the terror in her eyes as she realised her last request had not been adhered to. Within seconds she was lost within the mass of crackling flames. It is claimed that two or more officials collapsed into faints during the horror. Within three hours Elizabeth Fawson was no more, her body totally consumed by the fire. It seemed that her death had caused her as much suffering as her poor husband had undergone.

Shortly after her death the following letter was written by the local priest who had visited her in the condemned cell:

'Sir, the death of the unhappy Mrs Fawson gives me a liberty which before I had not of communicating to you some particulars relating to her, which may contain an answer to your enquiries, and which on the whole I did not think necessary to conceal.

The second time I visited her since she was under sentence of death she desired to speak with me alone; and then told me, that she could not be satisfied, till she had confessed to me, as she said she had done before to a worthy friend of mine, that she was indeed guilty of the crime for which she was to die. I took the freedom to ask her whether she were provoked to this unhappy action by an ill usage from her husband? She assured me with great earnestness that she was not and that during the time of their marriage she never received any unkindness from him. But the true reason was her uncomfortable affection for another person who was far from being in confidence with her on her attempt on Mr Fawson's life. I then mentioned to her what had been commonly reported concerning her falsehood on her husband's bed, and her being suspected of poisoning a fellow servant some time ago; but she solemnly denied both with repeated appeals to heaven as to her innocence, and seemed desirous that I would do her public justice as to both these charges if I had the opportunity.

I earnestly pressed her to make an open confession but she seemed utterly averse to it. She appeared heartily sorry for what she had done, and attended to religious instructions and prayers with great seriousness and many tears; but how far her repentance was sincere, genuine, and evangelical, He is only capable of judging before Whom she has now made her appearance, and from Whom she has received her final sentence.'

Amazingly it seems from the final paragraph that the priest himself did not feel Elizabeth Fawson's repentance to be authentic. The Church, like other organisations of the time, was dubious of a killer's sudden remorse. The knowledge, of one's own death caused the hardest of criminals to cry in fear of their anticipated fate, which was often a great deal worse than their actions as a criminal or killer. Hangmen were far from experienced or professional in their duties. There are recorded incidents of decapitation on the gallows, as well as of others lingering on the noose for almost 40 minutes before choking to death. The hangman was expected to kill the prisoner outright by breaking the neck but seldom did this occur, indeed it was more of a rarity.

# MURDER
# AT THE GATEHOUSE

NORTHAMPTONSHIRE has two villages named 'Ashton'. The one with which we are directly concerned is situated on the edge of the Ashton Wold estate near Oundle, tucked away in the north-east corner of the county. The village is somewhat remote and is only accessible via a narrow country lane which is marked by a typically old-style wooden sign, posted along the old Polebrook road. In 1952 the village consisted of just 32 thatched cottages, and to this day that same number are still the sum total of the village. The village was created around 1903 when Lord Rothschild had the cottages built in order to house the workpeople employed on his estate. In 1952 the estate was managed by Lord Rothschild's daughter, the Honourable Mrs George Lane and her husband, Mr George Lane.

George and Lilian Peach lived at a secluded cottage at the far end of the village, the cottage known as 'West Lodge' or the 'Oats House'. It was approximately 480 yards from the nearest cottage in the village. The couple had moved to Ashton in the spring of 1946. George Peach (known locally as 'Harry') worked on the estate as a gamekeeper/handyman. He was 64 years of age, his wife Lilian was 67 years old and the couple were liked by almost all the community, with no known enemies.

At 4.25 pm on Friday, 24th October 1952, George Peach said

goodbye to his old friend Walter Brundell in Ashton. The men had just finished a day's work and were on their way to their respective homes. Lilian Peach was seen hanging washing out at the cottage at around 5.00 pm the same evening. These were the last known sightings of the couple alive. The following morning, butcher's boy Lawrence Wright drove his van up to West Lodge in order to deliver the Peaches' Sunday joint. He entered the cottage grounds via the front gate and walked around to the rear of the cottage, where he knocked on the kitchen door. Receiving no answer, he tried the door but found it locked. Thinking that the couple were either out or had slept in, Wright decided to take the joint to the Three Horseshoes public house and leave it with Mrs Slater, wife of the licensee. As he got back into his van, Wright noticed that all the downstairs curtains were drawn across. On leaving the meat with the Slaters, Wright departed the village and returned to the butcher's shop in Oundle.

Frank Slater, licensee of the Ashton village pub, was rather concerned by the fact that there was no reply at West Lodge as he had heard that George Peach had failed to arrive for work earlier that morning. Slater walked over to the farm manager's office at Chapel Farm and asked John Dockray if he knew anything of George Peach's failure to attend work. Dockray said that he knew nothing about the matter but sent his secretary with Frank Slater to the cottage.

The publican found that the back door was locked but gained entry via the front door, which was closed but insecure. As he entered the house he called out to the Peaches but received no reply. Climbing the darkened stairs he peered into one of the bedrooms and instantly recoiled in horror, for there lying upon a bed was the bloody body of Lilian Peach. Breathing very heavily, she was unconscious but still alive. At once Slater retreated down the stairs and out of the cottage, returning to Chapel Farm where he telephoned the local police. The estate chauffeur was present when Slater made his frantic telephone call and returned to the scene with him as he was a qualified 'First-Aider'. The men took a cursory look at Mrs Peach and covered her until the arrival of medical assistance. There was no sign of George Peach in the room. Frank Slater checked the front bedroom but found it empty. The rear bedroom door however was locked. The chauffeur forced it open with his shoulder and both men were shocked by the sight which greeted them. Mr Peach lay in bed with the bedclothes pulled up around his neck. There was a large amount of blood on the left side of his head and pillow. He had been dead for some time, as rigor mortis had set in. Strangely the key to the bedroom door was not in position on either side of the lock and was never found.

Shortly after 11.00 am a doctor arrived, certified George Peach as dead and instructed that Lilian Peach be at once removed to Peterborough Hospital as she was in extremis. Inspector Harold Peel and Constable Moriarty of the Northamptonshire Constabulary arrived and made the normal initial examinations of the murder scene. It was noted that a small rear pantry window was open, with one of the tiny leaded panes missing, and this appeared to be the access point for the intruder/killer. Other than this there were no other signs of disorder within the house. Other senior officials arrived from the County Force and the whole area was more or less sealed off as a murder investigation commenced. At 7.45 pm that same evening Lilian Peach passed away in hospital. She never regained consciousness and thus never provided any clues as to the identity of her killer. Scotland Yard were requested to attend and duly arrived at Oundle police station at 11.00 pm that night and at once set up an incident room. The tiny community of Ashton could never have envisaged such an awful incident occurring, and one suspects would resent the publicity which it subsequently attracted!

It was discovered that the Peaches had a son (Jack) who lived and worked in Staines, Middlesex. Jack Peach knew nothing of his parents' murder until around 7.00 pm on Saturday 25th October, when local police officers called at his home to break the sad news to him. Jack had last seen his parents alive in mid August 1952 when they came to Middlesex to stay with him and his wife for six days. The shocked son travelled to Northamptonshire and had the awful task of identifying his parents' battered bodies in the mortuary in Glasthorne Road, Oundle.

Scotland Yard detectives made enquiries of all persons within the area. They confirmed that George Peach had received his pay packet on Friday 24th October, a sum of £9 13s 6d for that week. It was also ascertained that none of this money was spent yet despite exhaustive searches of the house no trace of this pay packet or money was ever found.

A post-mortem was carried out by Professor J. M. Webster of the Forensic Science Laboratory, Birmingham. He found that George Peach had sustained a number of heavy blows to the head and neck area causing the skull to fracture. Lilian seems to have struggled with her attacker as there was evidence of various contusions on different parts of her head where she had attempted to move her head away from the blows. There were also defensive wounds to her right hand and arm. It was stated by the professor that the probable weapon used in the attack was a hammer. He also believed that George Peach had been attacked between the hours of 1.00 am and 2.00 am on the morning of the 25th October.

Some 30 constables from Northamptonshire Constabulary were drafted into the village in order to carry out a systematic search in an attempt to locate the murder weapon. It was believed to be a coal hammer and it was confirmed that the outside coal shute door to West Lodge had been found open the morning the murder occurred. No stone was left unturned; gardens, outhouses and every possible nook and cranny was searched over the days which followed but there was no sign of the murder weapon. Thus detectives believed that the killer must have taken it away from the village.

The secluded, picturesque cottage of George and Lilian Peach, victims of a vicious attack in 1952.

Further mystery was created when at around 3.05 pm on 1st November 1952, Oundle police station incident room received a telephone call from a Mrs Marsh who resided at Chapel Farm House in Ashton. She had found a bloodstained hammer in the cabbage patch area of her garden. Superintendent Wilfred Tarr of Scotland Yard rushed to the house and took possession of the coal hammer. Apparently Mrs Marsh's daughter had lost her ring whilst playing in the garden; her mother went in search of it and found the hammer among fallen cabbage leaves, its head facing away from the boundary wall which actually fronts onto the main road through the village. The Superintendent identified matted hair and congealed blood on the head of the hammer and realised that it was very possibly the murder weapon. From the position of the hammer it was deemed that the killer had thrown it over the wall after committing the crime, yet the position where the hammer was located was some 600 yards from the Peaches' cottage. It would mean that the killer had carried the weapon past at least nine occupied homes! A stranger bearing such an object would. surely attract great attention.

Police enquiries moved to the nearby Polebrook Workers Hostel, whose many residents included Polish or other alien workers. A number of persons came under scrutiny at the camp but no-incriminating evidence against any was found. Enquiries were also carried out at the Molesworth aerodrome, where again a large number of contracted aliens were employed as well as servicemen from the USA, but there was nothing to arouse police suspicions of any such employees, with all providing accurate accounts of their actions on the night/morning of the crime.

The press reported that some 500 people had been interviewed. In reality the figure was closer to a thousand. Some 2,000 fingerprints (all male) were taken from local inhabitants in an attempt to match an alien fingerprint found on beading surrounding the broken pantry window at the murder cottage. None matched! The police seemed to be at a loss for clues or evidence. Various reports were received of a number of suspicious persons seen in the area around the time of the crime; a lorry driver reported that he had been travelling towards Wellingborough along the A605 road when as he approached Oundle he saw on a bend in the road some six persons, one of whom was a woman aged 40–45 years who ran into the road and attempted to stop the lorry. The driver swerved and was somewhat unnerved by the incident but continued on his way. He later claimed that the woman seemed to be agitated and in a desperate hurry to leave the area!

A railway porter from the North Station Peterborough reported sighting two suspicious men around 2.15 am on the morning of the murder. The men had entered the station via its main entrance. At 2.20 am he saw the men on board a King's Cross-bound train. Both men had flushed complexions as though they had rushed to make the train and one had tied a handkerchief around his left wrist, blood beginning to seep through the temporary bandage.

Once again these individuals were never traced and thus remain a mystery.

The police had released to the press that George Peach's pocket watch had been removed from the house. An accurate description of this watch was gleaned from an Oundle jeweller who had cleaned the watch for Mr Peach during the summer of 1952. The description was circulated in the *Police Gazette*. This in fact provided much conjecture, as on the afternoon of 8th November 1952 two men stood outside a jeweller's shop in Bedford High Street. One of the men entered the shop and requested that some repairs be made to the outer case of the watch. The manager made some brief adjustments to the item and handed it back to the men, who thanked him and left the shop but remained outside speaking to the second man and apparently examining the watch. Within a few moments he re-entered the shop and asked if the numerals on the face of the watch could be repainted. The manager advised him that this was not possible and once again the man left the shop, this time moving away from in front of the jeweller's with the second man. The jeweller described both men as rough roadster types who appeared to have been living rough for some time. The men were never traced nor was it confirmed that the watch concerned was that of George Peach. The mystery deepened by the hour and must have caused some concern to the investigating police officers.

The 13th November saw a minor breakthrough in the case when Detective Constable Lovell (Wellingborough) found a small flap-over style purse with thonged edges. The purse had been found on a grass covered bank on the left-hand side of the road leading out of Ashton, close to the farm manager's garden wall. This was approximately 800 yards from the scene of the crime and 125 yards from the site of where the murder weapon was located. The purse contained a single threepenny piece and was deemed to have been thrown onto the grass verge by someone leaving the village. The purse was later identified as the property of Lilian

Peach, though it remains a msytery as to why it was not found during the initial police search of the area. One can accept that not every blade of grass could be examined, but for the murder weapon and now other direct evidence to have been missed leaves much to be desired! But before jumping to conclusions as to the inadequacies of the police search, let us contemplate the fact that neither item may have actually been in situ during the initial search, but had been dumped by the killer after the event.

The police were baffled by the fact that there were no alien vehicle tyre tracks leading up to the cottage. All those evident were quickly traced and identified as local traffic visiting the scene throughout the day. Bicycle tracks were found and were soon identified as belonging to the cycle owned by William Underwood, the 65 year old village night watchman. Underwood had passed West Lodge at around 10.00 pm on the 24th October and had seen no sign of any lights from within the murder cottage. The estate chauffeur also clarified this point when he stated that he had passed the cottage at 11.00 pm and again saw no illumination from within West Lodge.

The press reported that the police had narrowed down a list of suspects and were now interested in just five men. Local newspapers ran such headlines as 'Is Northants Couple's Murderer Living In Locality?' Superintendent Tarr was quoted as saying that 'the murder may have been committed by someone living locally as there was no definite proof to the contrary.' Suddenly the enquiries took on a different complexion. The local people who had previously ably assisted police with all matters now became cynical of the whole affair. Many spoke to the press of their fears that the killer was still walking amongst them, part of their community. Womenfolk secured their front and back doors each time their men left the home for no matter what length of time. It seemed that a good number of the community were in fear of their lives.

George and Lilian Peach were buried in the graveyard of Fotheringhay church. Hundreds of people arrived at the church and a special bus was provided for the residents of Ashton in order that they could all attend to pay their final respects.

The police tracked every local man's movements on the night of the crime, and incredibly there were those who could provide little evidence of their whereabouts. What is odd about the whole affair is the fact that three estate workers living in the village had returned there at approximately 12.30 am on the morning of the murder. At least two of them had been out around the village for a further 30 minutes or so, yet neither had seen nor heard anything or anyone suspicious. Certainly neither could recall any further vehicular movement in the village up to the time they went to bed, though there was a somewhat spurious claim that a car had driven into the village and left some time later at high speed. There was no evidence of such a vehicle travelling along the dirt track road to West Lodge.

With little in the way of evidence, Scotland Yard returned to London, handing over the full details of the case to the local Constabulary who could ill afford to continue such enquiries for no other reason than lack of financial and manpower resources. A token force maintained their enquiries for a few days before it was felt that all lines of enquiries had been exhausted, the case was doomed to remain unsolved.

And so things remained until 4th October 1956 when Scotland Yard received an anonymous telephone call to the effect that a man on the fairground at Tottenham knew quite a lot about the unsolved murder in Northamptonshire four years previously. The police swooped upon the fair and 80 men were forced to provide fingerprints. The telephone call came from the Tottenham area, hence the police's belief that the allegation was accurate. The police remained at the fairground for some four hours before releasing staff and allowing them to continue as normal. It was recalled that a similar funfair was at Wellingborough during the week of the murder. Though the Tottenham fair had never actually travelled to Wellingborough, it was possible for some of its workforce to have worked there as they tended to change around quite a lot. The enquiries proved to be fruitless, none of the fingerprints taken matched the originals taken from the pantry window in the murder cottage. Hence the Ashton murder case remains unsolved.

Despite such a desperately disappointing result to the police enquiry all hope of catching the killer is not lost. Every so often the local press discuss the crime in some detail and conjecture that perhaps one day a death bed confession will reveal all. The official files disclose little in the way of real suspects though I am certain that the officers on the case had a fair idea as to a possible conclusion to the affair, but perhaps through lack of real evidence were unable to promote their suspicions any further.

I confess to siding with Superintendent Tarr in the belief that the killer lived locally; of this there is very little doubt. If the motive for the crime was burglary, then why was nothing within the house disturbed? Why would a burglar select West Lodge as his target when he would realise the probability of being sighted by someone whilst attempting to leave the village (which remember was almost a cul de sac)? Why murder the old couple who offered no real threat to a would be intruder? How would a stranger know his way through the house and why go apparently directly to the upstairs rooms?

There is much in the way of circumstantial evidence to support the theory that the killer was a local person – no tyre tracks, knowledge of the house, no strangers actually sighted in the area on the night of the crime, and finally the murder itself. The Peaches had to have been murdered with a purpose in mind, as they offered little physical threat on the morning in question to their attacker. Sadly, though, at this time that is all this theory is, pure supposition. Certainly I do not feel that I have written the last word upon the 'Ashton Murders'. Hopefully something or someone will one day end the years of speculation upon the county's most famous unsolved mystery!

# FOR THE LOVE
# OF LOUISA

NEVER in the annals of criminal history can there have been a more clear cut 'crime of passion' recorded as that which occurred in a sleepy Northamptonshire hollow in 1893.

The village of Burton Latimer is situated approximately two miles south-east of Kettering; today it is easily accessible along the A6 trunk road. It is a relatively long town with its quaint country cottages and houses reaching far beyond its present identified limits. The area has altered beyond recognition since the Victorian era with new housing areas and industrial developments springing up all over the place, yet it is still possible to identify the old town. It was this community which was devastated by an act of murder which is still recalled to this date.

Richard (Dick) Sabey was born in the village of Cranfield, Bedfordshire in the year 1845. He was a reasonably intelligent young man, having had a decent upbringing, and like so many young men of that particular era Dick Sabey enlisted in the British Army and was called upon to serve in such distant places as India and Africa. During his spell in India, Sabey met with and eventually married an Indian woman. After a full term of service in the army Sabey returned to his native country with his new spouse and child and settled in Leicester. His immediate problem was to find suitable employment, which was to prove no real concern to Sabey

Site of the Red Cow public house, now a hairdresser's, in Burton Latimer where the body of Louisa Johnson was taken and a post mortem carried out.

who was an excellent oral communicator, though his comments were often far from accurate. The Bedford Gas Company required various employees in certain areas and Sabey was able to procure such employment. He soon found himself disliked by many of his colleagues for expounding obvious untruths. He was also a bit of a womaniser. During the course of his employment Sabey was called upon to visit numerous homes during the normal working day, a time when the man of the house was normally absent thus allowing him to attempt to force his doubtful charms upon as many women as he could. It must be said that Sabey probably had more failures in his philandering than successes.

Sabey was called to a large house in the village of Cranfield, and whilst there he met Louisa Sophia Johnson, a pretty young housemaid who also hailed from Cranfield. Unlike Sabey, Louisa was somewhat naive in the ways of life and soon fell for Sabey's flattery and charm. Sabey showered her with cheap gifts and false attention. The gas worker deliberately kept from the girl that he was already married and so began a tempestuous and torrid affair enveloped in a shroud of deceit. Sabey convinced Louisa that his continued absences from Cranfield were due to his job, when in fact he was returning to his family home in Leicester. One wonders just what explanation he gave his wife?

It soon became clear to all that the little housemaid was with child and in due course she gave birth to Sabey's illegitimate child. Loyal to her lover, Louisa refused to reveal the identity of the father of the child, but tongues were beginning to wag and the accusing finger of guilt was correctly directed towards Dick Sabey, who began to suffer the wrath of the local people. Sabey suffered verbal and some physical abuse to such an extent that he volunteered to leave the area within a few days. However, like all true villains, he carried out one final devious deed before departing Cranfield; he persuaded Louisa to resign from her position in the village and to move to Liverpool with him. The lovers moved into rooms owned by a Mrs Peacock in the Merseyside city at a cost of five shillings per week. The landlady was sympathetic towards Louisa, possibly realising her naivety.

The trio lived together quite happily for two or three days until Sabey told Louisa that he had to return to the Midlands due to working commitments. He would remain away from Louisa for a few days, before returning with another pack of lies, and of course a similar scene was played out between Sabey and his wife in Leicester. The masquerade continued for several weeks until it finally began to cause a strain upon Sabey, both mentally and financially. The pressures he had placed himself under were now beginning to tell, his lies were becoming obvious to all the parties concerned. Eventually Sabey returned to Leicester and revealed the truth of the affair to his real wife, though whether this was a voluntary or forced confession is not known. Whatever the situation, Sabey had told the truth to his wife, who was none too pleased to hear it.

Early in the morning of 29th November 1892 the real Mrs Sabey arrived at the Liverpool rooms used by Louisa Johnson and child. The wife was quite obviously furious, she blamed the whole affair upon Louisa and accused her of encouraging her husband. Louisa was emotionally destroyed by the confrontation, which was the last thing she expected. Sobbing hysterically, Louisa made no reply to the viperous remarks rolling off Mrs Sabey's tongue. The aggrieved wife screamed 'Remember I am here now and if I catch you about with Dick again I shall give you a good hiding.' Richard Sabey cowered behind his wife, displaying his real cowardly nature, though every so often he would fire a barrage of abuse at Louisa then hide behind his wife again.

Amazingly, Mrs Sabey then attempted to persuade Louisa to part with her child in order that the Sabeys could adopt it, thus destroying all evidence of the affair. Louisa declined as politely as any mother could when receiving such a request and asked the Sabeys to leave at once. Desperate, Louisa turned to landlady Mrs Peacock for sympathy but the woman was more concerned about her rent money than Louisa and her sad plight. However, Mrs Peacock did assist Louisa in finding accommodation in a Liverpool workhouse where, in December of the same year, Louisa gave birth to a second illegitimate child from the relationship with Sabey. Already somewhat depressed by her surroundings, Louisa was distraught when her first child contracted an illness early in January 1893 and subsequently died.

As a last resort Louisa began to write to her married sister in Northamptonshire. Unlike Louisa her sister had married a steady and reliable worker by the name of Thomas Frederick Wright and lived in the picturesque IseBrook Cottage situated between Burton Latimer and Finedon. Correspondence flowed between the sisters and Louisa was able to profit from her sister's advice. An affiliation summons was taken out against Sabey, thus forcing him to provide some form of income for Louisa for the child's upbringing. Sabey was ordered to pay three shillings and sixpence per week to Louisa, an expense he could well do without as it caused him much grief with his wife who continually reminded him of his unfaithfulness. Louisa moved from the workhouse to IseBrook Cottage until such time as she was fully recuperated and able to find employment to support herself and her child.

Meanwhile Sabey found himself a virtual outcast within his own home. His extramarital affairs had caused his wife to harbour a deep distrust towards him, while he found it difficult to forget Louisa and believed that she still loved and desired him. Sadly Sabey could not have been more incorrect though a confused mind cannot clarify such attitudes. Dick Sabey decided to pay a final visit to Louisa in Liverpool and so on 6th February 1893 he left his Leicester home to go to Mrs Peacock's lodgings in Liverpool. Once again Sabey told his wife that he would be away for a couple of days due to his work and so began the first steps to disaster.

Sabey possibly believed that he would be able to persuade Louisa to drop the affiliation order against him and perhaps that he could have one final sexual encounter before dropping the girl. On arrival at Mrs Peacock's, Sabey was surprised to hear that the girl had moved into a local workhouse. He attempted to track Louisa down and soon realised that his journey to Liverpool had been a wasted one. Dick Sabey was angered by Louisa's actions, he felt humiliated by the fact that she had managed to make another life for herself without his knowledge. He decided to follow her down to Burton Latimer. Remaining overnight in Liverpool, Sabey must have dwelt upon the thought that Louisa had banished him from her mind. With his own mind in turmoil, Sabey entered a hardware shop in the city and purchased a sharp-bladed knife. The following morning he left Liverpool bound for IseBrook Cottage with murder on his mind.

On arrival in Northamptonshire, Sabey had great difficulty in locating IseBrook Cottage but eventually found it nestling close to the banks of the river Ise in superb country surroundings. Once there Sabey found himself unable to approach the cottage and so opted to lie in wait to confirm Louisa's presence there. It was not long before his patience was rewarded as Louisa emerged from the house carrying an empty pail in which to collect fresh water from the nearby Burton Mill. Sabey watched as Louisa carefully filled the pail and began her return journey. As she approached the cottage he stepped out and spoke with her. It seems that he was able to quell Louisa's initial fear of being alone with him, as soon the couple walked along the road away from the cottage towards Burton Latimer.

A local baker known as Edward Partridge called at IseBrook Cottage around the same time as Sabey and Louisa met. He claimed to have seen Sabey place his arm around the girl in a casual and relaxed manner and believed the couple to be quite content in each other's company. The baker was behind the couple when he met with some ironstone workers by the name of William and John Evans and James Burley. The group were strolling casually along the road towards their homes when they saw Sabey suddenly grab Louisa by the throat, forcing her head back. With his free hand he calmly produced a knife and sliced into the carotid artery. Blood spurted from the gash as Louisa somehow managed to yell 'Murder, he's trying to kill me', before breaking free of Sabey's grip, taking a few steps towards the group and collapsing in a pool of blood. Dick Sabey ran for cover behind a hedgerow in a field owned by a Mr Barlow. Thomas Wright emerged from the cottage to see what all the commotion was. He saw Louisa's lifeless body lying in the road and at once carried her back to the cottage, where he laid her upon a bed.

James Burley soon located Sabey and demanded that he come out from the hedge. Sabey did as was asked of him but refused to drop the bloodstained knife which he was holding, indeed he threatened the group with it. Thomas Wright approached Sabey who shouted to him 'Well, Mr Wright, she did it.' Wright

Richard Sabey was arrested and taken to the Gate Inn, Finedon (now the Tudor Gate, shown here) where he bought his captors a round of beer whilst awaiting the constable.

responded 'That's a lie, Dick.' Sabey then exclaimed 'Love did it.' The group were then shocked as Sabey offered Wright a sovereign. Thomas declined to take the money and Sabey then requested that he should send it to his (Sabey's) wife in Leicester; Thomas Wright agreed to do so. Sabey told the men that he had intended to do away with himself after Louisa but had been stopped from doing so by their intervention. None of the group believed him.

Before long a horse-drawn bus came along and was stopped by the men. The driver was asked to take them to Finedon in order that they could deliver the murderer to a constable. The bus carried the group to the Gate Inn, Finedon where captors and prisoner alighted and duly entered the hostelry. Once inside confusion reigned. Sabey purchased the group a round of beer whilst they awaited the arrival of the constable. A few minutes later Constable William Judge entered the inn, listened to the witnesses' testimonies and duly arrested Richard Sabey for murder. Once again Sabey denied killing Louisa and blamed the incident upon his undying love for the girl. This did not impress William Judge in the slightest, who with little emotion advised Sabey that he would be locked in Northampton gaol until the time of his trial. Sabey pleaded with the constable to have mercy upon him but once again Judge remained expressionless.

Richard Sabey was brought to trial at the Northampton assizes on 29th July 1893. His confession ensured that he was found guilty of murder and he was subsequently hanged at Northampton gaol two days later. On the morning of his execution a large crowd had congregated outside the prison walls, ballads were sung and the crowd rejoiced as the black flag was hoisted and the awful clanging of the death bell echoed around the prison walls. Among the crowd just one woman stood motionless once Sabey's death had been confirmed. She turned away from the crowd and made the lonely trip back to Leicester, in the knowledge that her husband's death was perhaps the best thing that could have happened to her.

Louisa Sophia Johnson was taken from IseBrook Cottage to the Red Cow public house in Burton Latimer, where a post mortem was duly carried out. An estimated 1,500 persons were present at Louisa's funeral in the tiny cemetery situated in Church Lane of the same town. Today the grave stands sheltered beneath the boughs of an elderly tree. An old rusting iron memorial plate stands at the head of the grave; long since broken it states:

'In affectionate remembrance of Louisa Sophia Johnson of Cranfield Bedfordshire.
Died 8th February 1893 aged twenty eight years.
The Lord has brought down my strength in my journey and shortened my days.

The memorial tablet above Louisa Johnson's grave. An estimated 1,500 people attended her funeral at the tiny cemetery in Church Lane, Burton Latimer.

Each of the locations mentioned within this case still exists. The Red Cow public house is now a hairdresser's situated in the centre of town just off the A6. The Gate Inn is still serving ale though under the new guise of the Tudor Gate. IseBrook Cottage still stands and is now slightly modernised but is still as picturesque, and finally the Burton Latimer cemetery stands in secluded Church Lane, Louisa's grave being immediately on the right as one passes through the old iron gates.

# POLICE KILLERS

WITHOUT doubt the most common type of murder is that committed through jealousy. The emotion of love is a powerful one and to interfere with such emotions is like conjuring up a recipe for dynamite! Domestic incidents between husband and wife or any couple residing together account for much of a police officer's work, though granted the majority of such incidents are quite tame compared to murder. Yet such is the case that once a police officer responds to such incidents he may suddenly become the villain of the piece. In some cases the disruptive couple suddenly join forces and turn on what they view as an outsider interfering with their lives! The majority of police officers fully expect this when responding to such incidents and it is true that most accept the criticism and abuse which occasionally comes their way on arrival at such a scene.

It is a fact that the good will, bravery and unselfishness of the police force in general is seldom appreciated and as such never has been. Dedication to duty is one of the set criterion required by the respective forces. Most police officers accept that violent attacks upon their person are part of their everyday duties and responsibilities, a common view is 'Someone has to do it'. Over the years literally dozens of police officers have been killed during the execution of their duties. Granted some were accidental deaths but others were clear cut cases of murder! The county of Northamptonshire, unfortunately, has quite a chequered history in this department.

Pattishall is situated just off the A5 trunk road to the south-west of Northampton. It is a picturesque little village dating back to the days of the Domesday Book, indeed a Saxon church still stands in the area. During the summer of 1789 Thomas Gordon, his wife Winifred and son Gordon moved to the village from London. Mr Gordon was a surgeon and apothecary and continued to practise in the Pattishall district. The Gordons were not a particularly friendly and sociable family and local opinion was that they had moved into the country in order to accumulate as much money as possible before returning to London.

The community of Pattishall found Mr Gordon obnoxious in his attitude towards village life while Mrs Gordon snubbed her neighbours and made no attempt to mix or participate in typical village community affairs. The 19 year old son was a natural agitator and liar. Over a few weeks the animosity between villagers and the Gordons increased, causing many violent altercations.

Police Constable George Linnell was the constable of Pattishall. He was well respected and one suspects that like many of his contemporaries of the time did not really relish his parish duties and responsibilities. Despite this he carried out his tasks in a most effective manner. Constable Linnell heard rumours of various physical assaults involving the Gordons, who were apparently the aggressors. A warrant for Mr Gordon's arrest was procured, though the sincerity of the charges made by local villagers is somewhat dubious. Constable Linnell left his home in the quiet village early one afternoon in late July 1789, his intention to arrest Mr Gordon on an assault charge. Calling at the Gordon house he was met by the uncouth Winifred Gordon, who claimed that her husband was absent from home on business. The Constable knew different but sensing a particularly volatile situation brewing he departed and called upon certain menfolk of the village for the purpose of entering the house by force if required to do so. Approximately one hour later Linnell and a few men returned to the house. Winifred Gordon and her son, who had a firearm, refused them entry. The action became frenzied. Stones and sticks were thrown at the house, breaking windows, and the Gordons came under a barrage of objects. The situation continued with the Gordons refusing to give way, until eventually Winifred Gordon screamed at her son to use the firearm. Thomas Gordon took aim and shot the advancing Constable Linnell dead!

At once the pandemonium ceased. It took a few moments for all to take in just what had occurred, then Thomas Gordon threw down the firearm and gave himself up to the men, who had him transported to Northampton to await trial. Winifred Gordon was also taken by the group as almost all had witnessed her instructing the boy to shoot the firearm at the crowd. Thomas Gordon was brought before Baron Thompson at the assizes and duly found guilty of murder. Winifred Gordon was charged with being an accessory to the crime and later received a minimal sentence for her part.

Thomas Gordon awaited execution in the condemned cell. He appealed against the punishment on three separate occasions and seemed to be having some success. Local opinion was that he would escape death, but the execution order was finally received and he was duly hanged at Northampton on 17th August 1789, his body afterwards being delivered to a surgeon to be dissected and anatomised. Amazingly public opinion of the time tended to side with Gordon, who was deemed to be an innocent party encouraged by his mother and his family loyalty. Little was said of the fate of the poor and unfortunate Constable Linnell who died whilst acting on behalf of the local community!

The next case took place in the town of Northampton some 79 years later. Once again the crime was nonsensical and involved an unfortunate police officer attempting to assist members of the public. James Kemp hailed from Birmingham and was born in 1837. He was a keen, athletically built young man whose only wish was for a successful career in order to support his family, which consisted of his wife, two children and elderly mother.

Victoria Street, Northampton, looking towards Campbell Square; scene of the shooting of James Kemp by William Bridgewater. Today's police station is in the background of the picture.

Kemp found the career he wanted when he joined the Birmingham City Police. All seemed to be going well for the Kemp household until his wife fell ill with bronchial problems. Doctors advised Kemp to move his family to a better environment in order to ease his wife's illness and so he transferred to the Northampton Borough Police and was quickly followed by his family. The fine Northamptonshire air tended to ease Mrs Kemp's breathing difficulties and the Kemp family enjoyed life in the rural community.

Experienced police officers were difficult to come by in those early days, and James Kemp was one of the few who possessed a fair degree of practical policing experience in different areas. Through his keenness and attitude, Kemp was made the first detective officer of the Borough, indeed according to an early Chief Constable's report he is titled as being a Detective Sergeant, though he is identified as being Detective Constable elsewhere. Whatever his rank, he was classed by all who knew him as a fine officer.

December 26th 1868 saw James Kemp on the 2.00 pm to 10.00 pm shift which in the main was uneventful. Having reported off duty Kemp left the police station and commenced his walk home. En route he met with two friends, George Crisp and Samuel Wills, who invited Kemp for a Christmas drink. Kemp knew it would have to be a quick ale as he wished to get home to his family at this time of year. Upon leaving the public house in Newland the three men entered Campbell Square. It was approximately 10.30 pm. Suddenly Crisp and Wills noticed a drunken man standing in the corner and heard another man shouting for assistance. Kemp thought it was a typical case of a drunken brawl and so walked over to the man who was standing in a waste area within the square.

As Kemp appproached, the man was heard to say, 'Keep away or I'll shoot you.' James Kemp was used to idle threats from drunken men, but suddenly the man raised both his hands and fired off a cartridge from a shotgun. He could not fail to hit his target from a few feet. The blast ripped into Kemp's left shoulder and neck area, tearing into the muscle and causing a wound which was believed to be some seven inches deep. With such injuries any normal person would have been killed instantly, not so James Kemp, who lived for a further three days before passing away.

The killer was one William Bridgewater, aged 28 years. Bridgewater had been suffering from bouts of depression since earlier in the year when he was forced to place his son into the custody of his father John at 3 Victoria Street, Northampton. Bridgewater had removed to Wellingborough where he had become lonely and subdued, resorting to heavy drinking sessions and generally ending the evening with a good old punch up with other drunken locals. Such was Bridgewater's situation that he had become mentally unstable and had threatened to kill himself on a number of

separate occasions. Bridgewater had visited his father and son at
Victoria Street on Christmas Eve. Also present at the house was
William's brother Henry. A third brother owned the Plumbers
Arms in Sheep Street, Northampton. Late on the evening of
Christmas Eve, William Bridgewater told his father that he was
returning to Wellingborough to do a bit of shooting!

Nothing was heard or seen of William until late in the evening
of Boxing Day when he returned to Northampton and visited the
Plumbers Arms, where he deposited a double barrelled shotgun
with his brother behind the bar. William seemed strangely agitated
and tense, though he was somewhat under the influence of alcohol. Leaving his brother's pub William visited Victoria Street and
entered his father's house, where the sight of his young son seems
to have thrown him into a frenzy. He demanded to take his son
back to Wellingborough. His father refused to allow the boy to
leave. A brief altercation transpired before William stormed out of
the house, slamming doors behind him.

William returned to the Plumbers Arms, grabbed his gun and
ordered a drink of ale. He talked of his distress at his father's
objections to allowing him to take his son. While William was in
the bar his brother Edwin ran to Victoria Street to warn his father
and brother Henry of William's threats. The house was secured
and the group within awaited the arrival of William, who now
appeared to be mentally unaware of his actions. William screamed
at the top of his voice for the front door of the house to be opened.
Henry Bridgewater opened an upstairs window and told his
brother to go away but William was in no mood for interference.
Without further thought he fired off the gun at his brother, only
narrowly missing him and blowing part of the ceiling out in the
upstairs room. In a state of sheer terror Henry fled the house as
William attempted to reload his gun. Screaming for the police he
ran to Fish Street police station. His screams had been those heard
by James Kemp's party, just as William Bridgewater had managed
to stagger into Campbell Square from Victoria Street.

After Kemp had been shot, Bridgewater fled back down Victoria Street to his father's home. John Bridgewater had heard the commotion and realised that his son had committed some heinous act and opened the door to him. William hardly had time to explain what had occurred when Samuel Wills, accompanied by Constable Dawkins from Fish Street police station, arrived and arrested William. For an hour or so William Bridgewater believed he had shot his brother Henry. He appeared to be mortified when he realised it was a policeman he had shot, and this was to be the basis for Bridgewater's defence at the subsequent trial on 10th March 1869. The jury returned a manslaughter verdict as opposed to murder, as it was claimed that Bridgewater was in such a state both mentally and physically that he could not differentiate between James Kemp and his brother! He was sentenced to 20 years penal servitude. Surely a more incorrect verdict can never have been found in a court of law; murder is murder, no matter who the killer thought he had shot.

James Kemp was buried on 4th January 1869 at the Billing Road cemetery. The inscription upon his gravestone reads:

'Erected by the municipal council of the Borough of Northampton
In memory of James Kemp detective officer, who died on the 29th December 1868 from the effects of a gunshot wound received while in the execution of his duty.
Aged 31 years.'

Our last incident takes us to the town of Kettering in the year of 1878. Just ten years after the sad killing of James Kemp a further incident occurred within the county resulting in the death of an officer.

David Davis was a Northamptonshire lad born in Welford in 1851. Davis was an enthusiastic young man and managed to obtain work as a labourer prior to joining the Northamptonshire

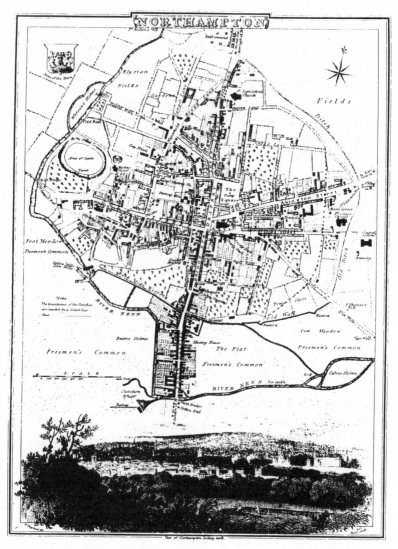

Map of Northampton in 1887 showing the old gaol clearly marked in black
below Abington Street.

County Force in June 1877. He was sent to serve at Kettering where he was quickly accepted as being a keen and efficient officer.

Davis had been in the force less than a year when at around 4.00 am on the morning of Wednesday 15th May 1878 he stumbled upon a man sleeping rough in an outhouse situated in Gas Street. The man was 45 year old Joseph Althorpe, a known drunkard and street brawler. Davis attempted to move the prostrate man but found it almost impossible. Eventually he was able to awaken the man and attempted to arrest him. Althorpe did not think twice, he scrambled to his feet, punching and kicking Davis as he did so. The unfortunate officer hardly had time to draw his truncheon, but had just managed to do so when Althorpe completely overpowered him and punched him to the ground. Suddenly the truncheon rolled free and the irate Althorpe grabbed it and began to club the defenceless officer over the back of the head and shoulders. Believing the officer to be dead, Althorpe fled the town, running across nearby fields.

Amazingly Davis was still alive and made his way back to Kettering police station, where he staggered into the main office and informed Duty Inspector Elijah Barwell of the incident before finally collapsing unconscious onto the floor with blood oozing from gashes in his head, neck and shoulders. After arranging treatment for Davis, the Inspector visited the site of the attack, which was a mere 400 yards from the police station. To his amazement a pool of blood was evident in the street where the attack had taken place and a steady stream of blood could be identified right back to the police station which was obviously Davis's route from the scene. All officers were warned of the attack and to be on the look out for Althorpe, who was now classed as highly dangerous.

The following morning he was to be captured in fields between Loughborough and Leicester and returned to Kettering and jailed awaiting trial. Althorpe was eventually brought before Mr Justice Fry at the Northampton Assizes on Wednesday 10th July 1878.

The authorities showed little or no compassion towards Althorpe, who displayed an arrogant and conceited attitude in the court during proceedings. As Davis had apparently survived the attack, Althorpe was charged with assault and received the extreme punishment of five years penal servitude.

The poor officer remained off work suffering from the results of the attack until Sunday 30th June, when he returned to what is classed as light duties (though in the police force, I hasten to add, there is no such thing!) on the professional advice of Doctor Dryland of Kettering. Just eleven days after his apparent recovery Davis was again taken ill complaining of severe pains in his head and arms. Living alone, Davis was advised to spend some time with relatives in Naseby, Northants, where a Doctor Hedley attempted to ease the officer's suffering. However, due to the severity of the internal injuries, Davis died early in the evening of 25th August 1878.

An inquest was held at the Fitzgerald Arms public house in Naseby where Doctor Hedley determined the cause of death as pericarditis. He also crucially added the fact that he felt he could find no connection between Davis's death and the assault in Kettering in May of the same year! Doctor Dryland was not so diplomatic, he stated a firm belief that had David Davis not received the injuries suffered in the attack he would never have died from the later illness. In other words he disagreed with Doctor Hedley, which was perhaps not medically ethical!

The authorities tended to side with Doctor Hedley and gave the cause of death as 'rheumatic fever', hence allowing a violent killer to escape punishment, as he was surely the main cause of blame for Davis's death.

In the early years of judicial history there are many such questionable verdicts by coroners and law courts, which occasionally tended to opt for the easy solution rather than discuss legal alternatives. The principal problem in this case was the fact that Althorpe had already been charged with assault and a punishment dealt out by the legal system, but such discrepancies should not allow a murderer to escape further punishment. Thus we have three rather controversial cases involving the deaths of serving police officers. In my own mind I believe all were murder, yet none of the offenders were charged with such. There is little left to say upon the matter but much to be thought!

# WHO KILLED SAMUEL OSBORN?

**P**ERHAPS the worst types of murder are those which seem to lack any kind of motive or reason and are by their very nature sickeningly horrific. Unfortunately such crimes fill the record books. They are those crimes which crime historians dislike covering. They may involve as a victim any person, yet historically children are a more obvious defenceless target. Next to children, the next most obvious targets are the old or the infirm. As one can appreciate, the killers of such victims are generally cowards, insecure and socially irresponsible.

Such a crime occurred in the market town of Kettering in 1886. Of all the towns within the county, perhaps Kettering has changed the most in the last century. The site of the fine Newlands shopping precinct has altered drastically since the 19th century when it was a maze of tiny courts and passages off Newland Street. It was in court 3 that 78 year old Samuel Osborn resided. He lived alone in one of two cottages within the court, the other cottage being occupied by the Ruff family – two sisters and one brother. A lamp was fixed to the corner of the Ruffs' cottage in order to illuminate the dark recesses of the courtyard.

Samuel Osborn was the archetypal Victorian character of literally dozens of towns similar to Kettering, a friendly genial character who worked hard all of his life to please others. He had lived in

Kettering for approximately 45 years having originated from Exton. For the few years leading up to 1886 he had kept himself busy by delivering handbills and timetables for the Midland Railway, for which he earned a modest weekly sum which was supplemented by an allowance of three shillings per week from the Kettering Board of Guardians. Locally known as 'Old Sam' he was a well liked gentleman with no known enemies. Sadly, though, his health was never robust. Those who knew him and often visited him were aware that he always left the outer door to his humble abode off the latch in order that when they called he would not have to get to his feet to answer their knocks.

On 24th December 1886, the son and granddaughter of Samuel Osborn were halfway along the passage leading from Newland Street into courtyard 3 when they met with Miss Ruff, who was a close friend of the family. Miss Ruff said to Samuel's son, 'I have just been in to see grandad to see if he wanted anything, and he is quite alright and comfortable.' Realising that his father was probably tired and resting the son decided not to call but to return the following morning in order to collect Samuel for the family's Christmas festivities.

The following morning the son returned only to be greeted by the sight of the Ruff family looking somewhat perturbed at the top of the passage. 'Something is wrong, we cannot open the door,' exclaimed the family. The son managed to force back the door and was met by a gruesome sight. There upon the concrete floor lay the battered body of his father in a pool of blood, his skull split open like a ripe horse chestnut. The bedroom to the cottage had been ransacked and it was an impossibility to confirm or deny that anything was missing. The Kettering police were informed and Police Sergeant Gilby arrived on the scene. He knew the family well and was sickened by the senseless crime. A search was made of the surrounding area in order to locate the murder weapon which was absent from the scene. It was believed to have been a 'chopper' (axe) but no trace could be found.

The police took away the chair on which Samuel had been sitting when the decisive blow was struck and the table nearby, though for what purpose is unclear, one can hardly see them as being ideal pieces of evidence. The police were at a loss as to why the attack took place. It was a common belief within the town that 'Old Sam' was penniless and that he had been on the parish (similar to social security) for a good many years. Sergeant Gilby made every effort to solve the crime and would not let it rest until his untimely death from smallpox a short while afterwards. The Osborn family were certain that when Gilby died every chance of apprehending the perpetrator of the crime died with him, for Gilby had spent countless hours questioning persons in the vicinity.

Almost immediately opposite the passage leading to the murder cottage stood a boarding house (Letts). Many unsavoury characters stayed there over a period of time and it seems that this sanctuary was the focal point of the police enquiries. Numerous persons were interviewed but none could throw any real light upon the crime.

On 29th December 1886 Samuel Osborn was buried at Kettering cemetery. Hundreds of mourners were present as the whole town was saddened by the pointless incident. Rumours were rife throughout the town as to identities of possible suspects and a few local rogues were apprehended and questioned but none could proffer any new information. Eventually a breakthrough seemed imminent when the news of an arrest was leaked a few weeks after the murder. John Sudborough, a 35 year old labourer who resided with a married sister (Mrs Barton) in Montague Street, was arrested and detained by the Kettering police. There were rumours that Sudborough and 'Old Sam' were not on friendly terms and there were numerous reports of altercations between the pair. To make matters worse Sudborough was seemingly boasting of some money which had recently come into his possession. He refused to divulge the origin of this money which caused people to suspect. Sudborough was released from police custody after several hours due to there being insufficient evidence to charge him. The local feeling was that Sudborough was the killer. He was rather an unsavoury character disliked by many, but despite this the police were not about to make him a scapegoat and chose to ignore public opinion, and were arguably right to do so!

As time wore on the case began to lapse from public memory until December 1905 when another breakthrough seemed probable. Apparently a convicted murderer who was known as 'Yank Perkins', a scoundrel who had killed Patrick Darkin in Newcastle earlier that month, had been executed in Newcastle gaol. Perkins originated from Northampton where he had a record of physical violence related to financial reward. It was believed that Perkins was in Kettering on the night of the murder and had in fact been staying at the 'Letts' lodging house. Information was received by the police that Perkins was the killer of Samuel Osborn and therefore a number of officers were dispatched to Newcastle goal in order that Perkins should be interviewed in the hope that he might actually confess to the crime. Perkins remained silent right up to his execution and possibly took his secret to the grave with him.

Amazingly much more evidence came out many years after the crime, though not of such importance as to point an accusing finger at anyone. Relatives of Samuel Osborn were invited to contact a local newspaper which had printed a picture of 'Old Sam'. A number of persons contacted the newspaper including friends and local residents at the time of the crime. It was ascertained by a family member that shortly before Christmas 1886, Samuel had asked his son to look after a few pounds for him. The actual sum was just under £5, but it was claimed by Samuel that he neither felt safe with the money nor his life. It was also believed that Samuel was to leave his home in the cottage after Christmas in order to move in with his son's family. During his early days Samuel had been a weaver and had a brother who lived in Oakham.

A friend who wrote to the newspaper claimed, 'It was generally supposed, after his wife's death, that as he still continued to live in the old cottage that he may have had money in his possession but no one who knew him would have taken advantage, because his whole support depended upon charity.'

And so the mystery of Samuel Osborn's strange death continues. Even today people about the town discuss the whys and where-fores of the story, and everyone has their own opinions as to the culprit's identity. Whoever killed Samuel Osborn was extremely lucky to escape justice. Certainly the missing murder weapon tends to the opinion that the crime was premeditated, but a stranger would find it difficult to lose such an item within the vicinity of the crime, certainly within a lodging house. And why did the attack take place? A stranger would hear little to attract him to Osborn's residence, even loose talk in a public house would hardly be likely to encourage someone to kill an old man who is known to survive on charity hand-outs. The killer perhaps was a local person who knew a little more about Samuel than we ever will, certainly there was some reason why the killer ransacked the bedroom after the murder. The prize indeed must have been a worthy one and not a hopeful burglary during which the intruder had been disturbed. We shall never know the real truth as to why Samuel Osborn was murdered that evening. I close with the words from Samuel Osborn's funeral card:

'In affectionate remembrance of Samuel Osborn, who died December 24th 1886.
The voice of this alarming scene
May every heart obey,
Nor be the solemn warning vain
Which calls to watch and pray. There is but a step between me and death.
(1 Sam xx3).'

# TOGETHER FOREVER!

RUSHDEN is a thriving industrial town situated on the A6 trunk road. It has long been renowned for its links with the bootmaking industry, which has long provided a source of employment within the area. Although the town is of a reasonable size and can be best described as sprawling, its residents some half century ago were extremely loyal and close knit. The events of 31st December 1942 caused horror and disbelief. Murder of any description is difficult to understand or believe, especially if the victim and killer alike are known to a society which perhaps was not used to such scandalous activities.

Arthur Clifford Sumpter had worked as a bootmaker and was apparently a very well respected member of the community. During the First World War he had been wounded and forced to return to England where he received expert medical attention from the staff of a hospital in the Tyneside area of the North of England. Sumpter was forced into a lengthy period of recuperation, during which time he befriended a colliery owner whose name was Embleton. Both men enjoyed each other's company, which greatly assisted Arthur Sumpter's recovery. After some time Sumpter was discharged from the services and returned to Rushden where he soon procured employment in the bootmaking trade.

In 1930 Arthur Sumpter received the sad news that his northern friend had passed away. To his surprise, Embleton had left him £30,000 in his will. Some months later Sumpter resigned from his position in the bootmaking industry and invested a percentage of

The public house where Sumpter and Gallay were last seen alive together on the night of the crime.

the money inherited in a large house on the Bedford Road. Sumpter was not a selfish person and invited his sister and brother-in-law to live with him. Mr and Mrs Frederick James Tyman assisted Arthur Sumpter with the general maintenance of the house, with Mr Tyman paying particular attention to the upkeep of the larger than average gardens, a task which he enjoyed. It would appear that the situation was an acceptable one for all parties concerned. Sadly though, all good things must come to an end. Arthur Sumpter had met with a young Higham Ferrers woman by the name of Betty M. Gallay. He invited the woman to move into his home and act as housekeeper. The summer of 1941 saw a split in the household; for whatever reason, Frederick Tyman and his wife moved out of Sumpter's home leaving him alone with Gallay. It seems that by this time Sumpter and his housekeeper were lovers.

Frederick Tyman would return to the house most mornings, making the couple breakfast and attending to other general tasks. Sumpter and Gallay would often laze about the house all day! Betty Gallay was on friendly terms with Frederick Tyman and often confided in him, telling of the problems she was encountering with 'Arthur'.

Betty Gallay had been spending more and more time away from Sumpter and perhaps there may have been those who knew of her relationship with a local soldier. Certainly Arthur Sumpter heard of these liaisons and was angered when he discovered that this individual had visited Betty at his house. An argument ensued but Betty Gallay was apparently more than able to pacify her jealous lover with some explanation or another.

Frequent quarrels followed and on Christmas Day 1942 came to a climax when Gallay told Frederick Tyman that she had informed Sumpter of her intention to marry her soldier friend. Tyman expressed his concern as to what Arthur Sumpter's reaction might be, but Betty Gallay explained that he had accepted the situation, offering little in the way of obstacles. The days which followed were to all intents and purposes normal, certainly there was nothing suspicious about Arthur Sumpter's comments or actions.

Thursday, 31st December 1942 started off as just another day in the life of Frederick Tyman. At around 8.00 am he arrived at the house on Bedford Road. He made a tray of tea for the sleeping couple upstairs before ascending the stairs, tapping on the couple's room door and leaving the tray for them. Tyman returned downstairs, tended to the boilers and checked over the winter damage to the garden before returning to the house and finding that Sumpter and Gallay had not stirred. Once again Tyman tapped on the bedroom door. Tentatively, he peered into the room and saw the couple lying on the bed on their backs. Betty Gallay's mouth was wide open. Tyman approached the bed and grabbed hold of Betty Gallay's hand, gently squeezing it in an attempt to awaken her. His ultimate fears were confirmed when he found that Gallay's hand was cold and stiff. It took a few moments for his senses to accept what he saw. A gun lay near Arthur Sumpter's leg and it initially seemed that both lovers were dead, possibly murdered!

Frederick Tyman wasted no time in telephoning the local police and advising them of his grisly find. It was around 10.00 am when Inspector H. J. Lee and Sergeant Tansley of the Northamptonshire Constabulary arrived at the house. The Sergeant was later to recall; 'The black-out curtains in the room were drawn, and the light was on. There were no signs of a struggle and Gallay lay on her back with her arms folded over her chest. Sumpter was also on his back with his head resting on the woman's shoulder. Two inches from his right hand was a .38 Service Enfield revolver.' Doctor Lean of Rushden was summoned and confirmed that Arthur Sumpter was still alive though very ill. He also ascertained from various tests that Betty Gallay had been dead around six hours.

Medical examination confirmed that Betty Gallay had sustained four independent bullet wounds, three to the chest and one in the arm. Any one of the wounds in the chest region could have been fatal. It seemed certain that the murder weapon had been the service revolver which lay next to Arthur Sumpter. The wounded man was transported under police escort to Northampton General Hospital where he died several hours later without regaining consciousness. Two bullet wounds were found in his body, one in the right temporal region which had been fatal and another in his left shoulder.

The immediate problem facing detectives was just who had committed such an horrendous act? A search of the house revealed very little, though it was confirmed that there was no evidence of a break-in. Numerous persons were interviewed but not one person could confirm any sighting of suspicious individuals in the area the night before.

It was to be judged from forensic and medical evidence that the incident had been a case of murder then suicide. From the positioning of the bodies it was clear that Arthur Sumpter had been the last one to be shot, therefore it seemed likely that he had shot Betty Gallay before killing himself.

The inquest was held at Wellingborough Petty Sessional Court on Saturday, 6th January 1943 with East Northants Coroner Mr J. Cairns Parker presiding over affairs. Mrs Laura Barratt informed the court that Betty Gallay was her daughter. Laura Barratt explained that shortly before her daughter's death there had been a serious and emotional quarrel between the couple, resulting in Betty returning to her mother's home. Apparently she had found a written note from Sumpter in which he stated that he was going to kill her before ending his own life.

Inspector Lee took the witness stand and advised the court of what he believed to be the full story of events leading up to the incident. The couple had been sighted in a public house in Wymington at approximately 10.00 pm the night prior to the crime. On returning home Gallay had told Sumpter of the precise nature of her relationship with her soldier friend. Sumpter, it was claimed, calmly accepted this and managed to encourage Gallay to partake in a measure of whisky with him in her room. Betty Gallay had eventually laid upon the bed and possibly requested that Sumpter leave her to sleep. This he did without further objection. Entering his own room (the couple slept in separate rooms), he took the revolver from the wardrobe and went to bed. Some time later he returned to Betty Gallay's room and fired the four shots into her defenceless and possibly sleeping body. He had then climbed onto the bed beside her and shot himself. In order to confirm much of this story the Inspector produced certain letters which tended to substantiate the theory in one way or another. Cartridges matching those found in Sumpter's revolver were found next to the body of Betty Gallay, thus proving that Sumpter's firearm was indeed the murder weapon. A further 24 cartridges of a similar nature were found in Sumpter's wardrobe.

Coroner Cairns Parker informed the jury that it was their

decision as to whether the police inspector and other authorities which corroborated his assumptions were accurate with these theories. The jury took little time to agree with the authorities and their verdict was murder followed by suicide. Arthur Clifford Sumpter had committed cold blooded murder. It was an obvious crime of passion dictated by Galley's relationship with her soldier friend. From the evidence available it would seem that Arthur Sumpter found it difficult to comprehend just why or how his loved one could reject him and the financial security he offered. This rejection ultimately drove him to murder; a torrid and tempestuous relationship destroyed a 44 year old bachelor and his 24 year old housekeeper, neither of whom can be directly blamed for the circumstances within which they found themselves.

Despite the decision of the coroner's court there remain several mysteries which have not been satisfactorily resolved. The main question is, why was Sumpter shot in the shoulder? It is possible that Sumpter was highly intoxicated on the night in question. After shooting Betty Gallay (in haphazard manner) he then turned the gun upon himself, and perhaps accidentally the gun went off, wounding him in the shoulder? It would take great determination and strength to then take aim again (and one must wonder whether an intoxicated man could do so) but this seems to be the only straightforward explanation. The alternatives are far too complex and would tend to differ from the documentary evidence available. The deaths of Betty Gallay and Arthur Sumpter show how the emotion of love, enflared by alcohol, can cause one person to carry out the unthinkable. A truly unfortunate crime.

# THE
# FARMYARD MURDER

OF all the motives for murder perhaps the most obvious is
that of the crime of passion. Generally they are sad affairs
revolving around emotional stress brought about by lust
or jealousy. Normally when such crimes occur the investigating
authorities have an easy task in providing a solution to the
incident; it is a recorded fact that a high percentage of murders are
committed by some person who is emotionally close to the victim.

The village of Charwelton is situated close to the western border
of Northamptonshire approximately seven miles from Daventry.
Unfortunately today there is little left to remind us of the prosper-
ous community which flourished during the Middle Ages. All that
remains of the original settlement is an ancient church and a
couple of homesteads (one of which is a farm, the other being a
cottage). The old village is today known as Church Charwelton
but little exists to determine its precise boundaries within the
community.

At some time in the 16th century a rambling farmhouse was
erected on the outskirts of Charwelton along the Priors Marston/
Hellidon road. The house was aptly titled Cherwell House and was
perhaps one of the largest houses within the community at that
time.

In 1821 the farmhouse was owned by a wealthy farmer by the

name of John Clarke who was 67 years of age. His wife Mary was a mere 35 and perhaps understandably she was dissatisfied with her lot. Her ageing husband had never offered her much in the way of excitement, he seemed too infatuated with his farming, and perhaps Mary felt like an ornament, receiving little or no attention. However, unknown to John Clarke his wife had for some time been having an illicit relationship with a farm labourer by the name of Phillip Haynes. This relationship was of at least seven years standing yet had remained a closely guarded secret. Indeed so clandestine had the relationship been that at one stage prior to Mary's marriage to John Clarke, she had given birth to an illegitimate child which was farmed out to close friends of the mother. Unfortunately the child contracted some illness and died within one year. Shortly after this Mary moved into Cherwell House with John Clarke as his mistress, a position which did not greatly please her but allowed her some form of financial reward as she used her affluent partner's hard-earned money for her own purposes.

One morning after a violent argument had taken place within the farmhouse, Mary left Clarke and ran away to Northampton. She could bear no more of his elderly mannerisms and idiosyncrasies, and it seems probable that Clarke had found out that Mary was using him for his wealth. However, he was not prepared to lose the object of his desires so easily and together with his friend Edward Turland he managed to locate Mary and persuade her (through a marriage proposal) to return with him to the farm.

Marriage meant that Mary was officially heiress to all of Clarke's estate, a proposition which she could not refuse. After discussing Clarke's proposal with her lover Phillip Haynes, the pair decided that it would be best for her to marry the farmer; upon his death they could then marry and secure a good lifestyle for themselves.

The marriage therefore was little more than a sham. Two children were born, though it is difficult to imagine just who the real father of these may have been. Mary requested that her

# A Copy of Verses,

## ON THE UNFORTUNATE MAN AND WOMAN

# *Phillip Haynes,*

### AND

# Mary Clarke,

Who was Executed at Northampton March 10, 1821

### FOR THE

## Wilful Murder of John Clarke,

*Husband to the latter at the parish of Charwelton, Northamptonshire.*

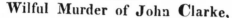

Good people all of each degree,
Give ear unto my tragedy,
Which I am going to unfold,
It is as true as e'er was told.

At Charwelton Northamptonshire,
A wealthy farmer lived there,
One Mr. Clarke he had a wife,
But lived a most unhappy life.

His wicked wife we understand,
Connected got with her servant man.
One Phillip Haynes that was his name
From Adstone, Northamptonshire, he
came.

Their intimacy it got so,
That all her secrets let him know,
Persuading him day after day,
To take her husband's life away.

Then this unfortunate Phillip Haynes,
For carnal lust and cursed gains,
Soon yielded to her cruel will,
Her husband Mr. Clarke to kill.

Then unto Brackley he did steer,
Into a shop he entered there,
He bought a gun, powder and shot,
To execute the cruel plot.

To Mary Clarke he did return,
Who's heart with cruelty did burn,
And told her he had obeyed her rules,
For he had got the fatal tools.

To scheming then they did proceed,
The safest place to do the deed,
Says Haynes I'll go into the barn,
For there no one can me discern.

Or where I am no one can tell,
Says Mary Clarke that's very well,
For there in secret you can stay,
Amongst the barley night and day.

Until that you have done the deed,
I'll bring you every thing you need,

So back and forward Haynes did go,
Unto the barn as you shall know.

From February the 8th day,
Until the 10th Haynes there did stay,
When Mr Clarke without regard,
Then came into the hay rick yard.

Then straight upon the rick he got,
When from the barn Haynes at him
shot,
Which gave to Clarke his mortal wound,
And brought him soon unto the ground

And as upon the ground he lay,
I'm done, I'm done, Clarke he did say,
When cruel Haynes heard him say so
He knew he'd gave the fatal blow.

Then this vile murderer he did creep,
Into the barley mow so deep,
Thinking to get out of the snare,
But soon he was discovered there.

Then he confessed the cruel deed,
And to Northampton sent with speed,
So now we'll leave him there to mourn
And unto Mary Clarke return.

Who in short time she taken were,
And lodg'd with Haynes to take a share
For their sad act of cruelty,
while blood for vengeance loud doth cry

At the assizes they were brought,
To answer for their cruel fault,
The Jury soon did guilty cry,
And they were both condemned to die.

And on the 10th of March they were,
Brought up the awful fate to share,
That day upon the gallows tree,
They suffered for their cruelty,

Now let their fate a warning be,
To all of high and low degree,
Be constant to your bosom friend,
Then God will bless you to the end.

T. Bloomer, Printer, 42, Edgbaston Street, Birmingham,

A 19th century broadsheet with the tale of the execution of the ignominious pair Mary Clarke and Phillip Haynes, for the murder of John Clarke.

mother be allowed to reside at the farm in order to assist in raising the children, John Clarke agreed and soon the women were dictating the farmer's affairs.

In February 1819 Mary persuaded her husband to employ Phillip Haynes as a general labourer upon the farm. The farmer was suitably impressed by the labourer's hard work, but was also quick to notice just how much attention he was devoting to being close to Mary. Without further ado Clarke sacked Haynes and evicted him from the room he had provided. Surreptitiously, Mary contacted her close friends John and Elizabeth Bush at Byfield, and arranged for Haynes to lodge with them until further notice. Elizabeth had been a personal friend of Mary for some considerable time and had been present at the birth of her 'official' children. Elizabeth remained loyal to her friend and paid frequent visits to Cherwell House, discreetly passing letters between Haynes and Mary. These were not just ordinary letters, some were ideas for murder. Mary Clarke was now desperate to rid herself of her husband. Natural death could take years, which was too long for Mary to wait; her husband had to be killed as soon as possible.

Phillip Haynes was so besotted by his lover and perhaps greed at the thought of inheriting the farmer's lot that he was prepared to do anything, even murder, if the need arose. Haynes possessed the typically scheming and cunning mind of a killer. He realised that John Clarke's death must appear to be accidental in order that suspicions could not arise against Mary or himself. It was obvious that some questions would be asked, but as long as the death was not obviously connected to him, he was in the clear. Phillip Haynes made three unsuccessful attempts at murdering John Clarke, each attempt was pathetic to say the least and displayed the classic symptoms of cowardice.

The first attempt at murder came late one night. John Clarke was returning home alone after visiting friends in a nearby village. His horse was galloping at high speed, and as the animal turned into a small copse close to Cherwell House, Clarke felt a stinging blow to his chest and was thrown backwards from the saddle. Shaken he rose to his feet and peered into the darkness. There he noticed a rope which had been tied between two of the trees at the entrance to the copse. The rope was chest height and could have proved fatal had it made contact with his throat. Without realising that an attempt had been made on his life, Clarke cut down the rope and made his way home, possibly in the belief that local brigands had placed the rope there in order to commit robbery. The following morning John Clarke spoke of the incident with other local people and warned them of the possibility of being attacked by rogues who appeared to be in the area!

Mary Clarke was furious with Phillip Haynes and his half hearted effort at murder. He would have to be much more cunning and courageous if he really wished to take the farmer's place. Phillip Haynes told Mary that her husband would soon be dead.

Late one winter evening in 1820 a second attempt upon John Clarke's life was bungled. Haynes laid in wait by a gated wall close to the farmhouse. In his hand was a large wooden club he had manufactured for the purposes of murder. It was not long before the unsuspecting Clarke came by the gate and without warning he was clubbed to the ground from behind. Stunned, he attempted to see his attacker, but his vision was obviously distorted as he was to later describe the person as being short and wearing a red striped waistcoat. Haynes was a tall slim character and amazingly was never suspected by Clarke. Within days of this, Haynes had purchased some poison (laudanum) and sent it to Mary in order that she should add it to her husband's tea. However, the poison was not administered in strong enough doses and merely made John Clarke sick!

Mary now urged her lover to act with haste and to make a determined effort at murder. She explained that if he was to purchase a pistol he could shoot Clarke and escape detection by fleeing the scene. Initially Haynes declined to take part in any such act but eventually he purchased a horse pistol, some large shot and a quantity of gunpowder from a shop on Market Hill in Brackley. On the morning of 8th February 1821, Phillip Haynes plucked up the courage to try yet again to kill John Clarke.

Haynes climbed into the hen roost in the barn close to the farmhouse. From this position he could get a clear view of everyone who came and went through the farm buildings. The hesitant killer made a small den for himself amongst the hay and was provided with food and drink by his lover. Haynes once again became conscious of what he was being asked to do and found himself unable to complete the task, but Mary continued to goad her lover until eventually, at about four o'clock in the afternoon of Saturday 10th February, Phillip Haynes fired the shot which killed John Clarke. The farmer was hit below the elbow and on the upper left arm. The initial wound was so large and exposed that the doctor could easily insert his fingers into it and feel the splintered bone!

Badly wounded, John Clarke was forced to retire to his bed. The surgeon was called from Badby and advised that the arm had to be amputated before gangrene set in. The farmer realised his days were numbered and immediately requested that his will should be completed in order that his affairs were settled on his death. The surgeon agreed to delay the operation whilst this was carried out. Once the operation had been completed the limb was examined and traces of lead shot were found in the bone. A cursory search of the farm's outbuildings was made with little effect. Phillip Haynes remained in hiding amongst the hay in the barn; there was no escape from his place of sanctuary until such time as the commotion surrounding the attack had subsided.

Anthony Marriott, a labourer on Clarke's farm, was present when his master was shot. He recalled a puff of gunsmoke coming from the loft in the barn. Due to the commotion at the time he had temporarily forgotten about this and afterwards when he had recalled it he felt it was too late, as the outbuildings had already been searched with negative results. But on Monday 12th February, Marriott decided to carry out another search of the barn and in particular the hay loft, tentatively prodding the hay with his pitchfork. Marriott's heart bounded when something stirred beneath the hay. He prodded the fork with some force into the area where he felt someone was hiding, and suddenly Haynes, who was known to Marriott, stood up and exclaimed 'Be civil and I will stand up.' Marriott replied 'You rascal, I have a good mind to stab you – you did not mind killing my master.' Haynes was taken prisoner but prior to him being taken away John Clarke requested to see him. Haynes was led into Clarke's bedroom, where the injured man pointed at him and said 'You bloody minded fellow, how could you do me such an unkind act?' Haynes denied the shooting but his presence obviously irritated Clarke, whose condition worsened so much that he died at four o'clock the following morning.

Some lead shot and an incriminating letter from Mary Clarke were found in Haynes's coat. A search of his lodgings at Byfield revealed further letters between both parties which contained damning evidence as to their apparent guilt. Mary Clarke was not arrested for a further week as Haynes continued to deny all knowledge of the crime and claimed that he was an innocent party who had been framed by someone else.

The pair were brought to trial at the Northampton assizes and were correctly found guilty of murder. Prior to their execution on Northampton Heath, both confessed to the crime and repented their sins. Mary Clarke was visited in the condemned cell by her two children and it is claimed that the sight of them made her guilt-ridden, hence her confession. A large crowd witnessed the execution and both prisoners seemed agitated by the thought of their fate.

Cherwell House, the scene of this dreadful crime, was demolished in 1978 and a new farmhouse has since been built close by.

# THE
# PECULIAR CASE
# OF MISS LYDIA ATLEY

THERE can be nothing more intriguing than a typically old fashioned English murder case, especially when it possesses all the criteria one would expect from an Agatha Christie novel. Seldom is murder as dramatic as depicted by fictional crime writers who tease their audience with snippets of information which are meant to deepen the plot and mystify one and all. Yet fact proved to be stranger than fiction in the incidents which took place in the tiny community of Ringstead in 1850.

Ringstead is situated in East Northamptonshire between the towns of Raunds and Thrapston. Ringstead now has a population of around 1,300, but in the mid 19th century it had no more than a hundred or so, a typical small community where everyone knew everyone else's business. In the main the tittle-tattle was not of the malicious kind occasionally found in small communities but more of a good natured banter concerning local folk. As is the case in so many small communities certain individuals receive more local attention than others; in Ringstead the individual was Miss Lydia Atley, who was a weak-minded young woman in her late twenties. Lydia had been forced to make her own way in life due to the death of both her parents and to her credit she worked hard at cleaning chores for local families, which endeared her to most village folk. Not being the most attractive of young women she found male companionship difficult to acquire. It came as some surprise then when she announced to her close friend that she was with child.

Typically the news within the community was met with much inquisitiveness as to the identity of the father. Lydia remained tight-lipped for many days until eventually she found the pressures forced upon her too great to bear and revealed the father to be none other than William Weekley Ball, a local butcher who to all intents and purposes was a happily married man. Ball denied the allegations in order to maintain stability within his own marriage but there is little doubt that there had been a relationship between the couple, who were regularly sighted together walking through local village lanes. Ball had told Lydia that he intended to leave his wife and that he wished to marry her. Initially Lydia had believed him but now she had announced the impending birth Weekley Ball had become evasive and refused to see or speak with her. Some-time around 20th July 1850 Lydia visited her close friend Mrs Groome. She advised her confidante that she desperately required some money and that it was her intention to get this from Weekley Ball. It would seem probable that this money was to subsidise an abortion, as Lydia spoke of wishing she had never met with her lover or allowed herself to succumb to his manly charm! Mrs Groome was concerned about her friend, who was extremely agitated and disillusioned. After a long talk on the matter Lydia left, explaining her emotions at the realisation of Weekley Ball's empty promises of marriage. This was the last Mrs Groome was to see of her friend, as one of the most mysterious incidents ever to occur in Northamptonshire took place.

Early in the evening of 22nd July 1850 John Hill, a local farmer, saw Ball and Lydia stroll into the orchard area of the butcher's garden. The couple seemed as though they were in dispute and Hill thought nothing more of it as he had no wish to cause any further grief for young Lydia by adding to the already rife gossip about the relationship. Suddenly, without warning, Hill heard Lydia shout 'I won't, I won't, it's yours and nobody else's.' The inquisitive farmer attempted to peer through the thick hedgerow which surrounded the orchard but found it impossible to see anything.

A short time later Joseph Groome, husband of Lydia's closest friend, was out walking in the village when, on passing the same orchard garden, he overheard part of a conversation involving Lydia and Ball. Lydia said 'I believe you mean to kill me Weekley Ball, Lord have mercy upon me if I am to die in this condition.' Mr Groome decided to ignore the statement as little more than an inaccurate accusation from one lover to another, though he did feel strongly enough about it to inform his wife, who also felt it to be an idle threat.

Perhaps no more would have been said of these incidents had matters not drastically altered, for Lydia Atley disappeared from the face of this earth that very same July evening, John Hill being the last local person to see her alive, with the exception of her murderer.

Initially the local opinion was that Lydia had received a sum of money from Weekley Ball in order to leave the area and enable her to begin a new life with her child elsewhere. Without commenting too deeply upon this topic, Weekley Ball appeared to encourage these rumours and said he had no idea as to where Lydia had gone to, the obvious inference being that she had moved location. As with any solution to mysteries there were the sceptics who refused to believe that Lydia would simply uproot and leave the district overnight, and soon rumours of murder were prevalent, with the blame being laid firmly at the door of Weekley Ball. Over a period of a few days Weekley found his once successful butcher's business floundering as the local community made their suspicions obvious. Ball was ignored locally wherever he went. To add to his torment his wife had to suffer those patronising smiles and secretive whispers which are always evident when a certain type of person feels they have an advantage over someone else, especially when it is something like murder!

The escalating rumours increased in fury and soon came to the attention of the local authorities, who were concerned by the accusations made against Weekley Ball. One of the strongest beliefs was that Weekley had murdered Lydia, then buried her remains in a new grave in the Meeting Lane cemetery. This theory seemed quite plausible as a grave had been dug in the cemetery the day prior to Lydia's disappearance. The authorities investigated matters and examined the grave where just one body, that of the lawfully dead person, was found, but still the rumours persisted until finally Weekley Ball was arrested and charged with murder. The accused man was adamant as to his innocence. He claimed that he was the victim of circumstances and village gossip. After all, he said, how could he be guilty of murder if no body had been found? The local magistrate at Wellingborough concurred with these sentiments and duly released Weekley from his confinement. The local community were irritated by this – to their mind the butcher was a murderer despite the fact that no body was yet found.

With his butcher's business in ruins Weekley Ball left Ringstead with his wife and purchased a new shop and home in Ramsey, Huntingdonshire (now Cambridgeshire). There business prospered and once again his home life became settled. At last he was able to forget the recent tortures of Ringstead.

But life is not so straightforward. The people of Ringstead still harboured a grudge against Ball and as such refused to let matters drift from memory. Every effort was made by those very persons who saw Ball as a killer to locate Lydia in neighbouring counties. Eventually the whole community came to the conclusion that Lydia Atley had been murdered, as not one solitary person could recall seeing anyone matching her description leaving the area on the night in question, and one must come to the conclusion that she would have encountered *someone* had she attempted to leave the area. Realistically Lydia or her remains must still be in the area.

Over the decade which followed there were various theories as to Lydia Atley's fate. There were those who believed that the butcher had chopped the woman into small pieces and sold her as meat in his shop. Others felt that she was buried within the orchard garden. People were allowing their imaginations to run wild, thus adding further mystery to what was rapidly becoming something of an enigma for the authorities.

Some 14 years later on 13th February 1864, a group of local labourers were busy clearing ditches around the Ringstead area when in Keystone Lane they happened across what appeared to be human skeletal remains. This fact was soon confirmed when the remains were also declared to be those of a young female. One of the labourers claimed that it was the skeleton of Lydia Atley. He was able to positively identify her by virtue of one of the lower teeth being absent from the skull's lower jaw; the tooth, he claimed had been pulled from Lydia's mouth personally by him. Once again the authorities were alerted and Weekley Ball was again arrested and charged with murder. After a two day hearing before Thrapston magistrates, Ball was committed for trial at Northampton's March assizes (25th February 1864) and a case consisting of mainly circumstantial evidence was compiled against him.

It was just over one week later when the same group of labourers found a second skeleton close to where the original was located. The second remains were identified as being male. Two further skeletons were found on 7th March and it soon became clear that unless Ball was a serial murderer who buried each of his victims in the same area, which he most certainly was not, then the skeletons were nothing to do with Lydia Atley's disappearance. The trial at Northampton was terminated and the charges against Ball dropped. The mystery of the skeletons was soon resolved when it was recalled that a gipsy encampment had been present in that area some years before and it was known that they had buried some of their dead around the camp site. Meanwhile Ball returned to Ramsey, but soon realised that the scandal caused by his arrest had once again destroyed his reputation. He sold up his business and returned to Ringstead, where the rumours continued until long after his death many years later.

With Weekley Ball dead the mysterious disappearance of Lydia Atley could be expected to be forgotten, especially so as most of those involved had also passed on. However life (or death as it may be) occasionally plays a cruel hand and on 25th July 1906 the quiet community of Ringstead was buzzing in anticipation. There were rumours of another skeleton having been unearthed in the locality. A local farmer by the name of Tilly had employed a farm worker (Mr Mayes) to dig out gravel from some of his fields along

Labourers clearing these ditches in 1864 uncovered human skeletal remains initially thought to be those of Lydia Atley.

the Thrapston Road. Mayes was making good headway with his task when suddenly the blade of the spade he was using struck something hard approximately eight inches below the surface of the soil. Clearing away the mud and grime Mayes peered curiously at what appeared to be a large cream rock. Tentatively he moved the object with the spade and as it rolled back he saw that it was a human skull!

Mr Tilly the farmer arrived and both men cleared the area surrounding the find until it was quite clear that it was the remains of a human skeleton. Close by the men found what appeared to be the blade and part of a handle of an old style razor. The village constable (Mr Sullivan) was summoned to the scene. Upon his arrival a large crowd had gathered and the topic of conversation was once again Weekley Ball and Lydia Atley. The astute constable ensured that the remains were protected from prying hands and sent for Doctor Buckley of Thrapston, who was to confirm that the remains were those of a woman aged between 26 and 30 years. A report was submitted to coroner Mr Parker who declined to open an inquiry due to the lack of positive identification! It seems almost certainly caused by severance of the carotid artery by virtue of the blade found close by.

But who was her killer? Or could she have committed suicide? It is now almost impossible with any degree of certainty to prove or disprove the identity of the killer, but circumstantial evidence must play a large part in any such investigation. Initially we can forget suicide. The body must have been buried in a shallow grave at the time of the disappearance otherwise it would have been found long before. Secondly, why would Lydia walk to that particular place in order to kill herself, surely she could have done so in the privacy of her own rooms!

Let us look at the circumstances which were occurring in the village around the time of Lydia's disappearance. The only person who could profit from Lydia's death was Weekley Ball; his marriage would again be secure and his standing in the community could once again be confirmed. One must remember that prior to the anouncement by Lydia, Ball and his wife were respected members of the community. The pressures brought about by the embarrassment of his predicament were enormous in such a small community. Weekley Ball awoke one morning to find his life in ruins, leaving the area could provide no reasonable solution. In desperation, I believe, on the night of 22nd July 1850, Ball and Lydia met in his orchard garden. The purpose of the meeting was twofold. Initially Lydia required money to subsidise an abortion, but prior to asking for this did she wish to make Weekley suffer to the extreme by persecuting him until he would be only too pleased to provide her with the funds she required? Weekley on the other hand may have questioned Lydia as to her promiscuity and why she felt he was the father. Certainly the comments overheard by Mr Groome and Mr Hill would tend to confirm this point.

Weekley Ball would by this point be a desperate man, his life destroyed by what he now saw as a foolish young girl with no responsibilities. It seems likely that Weekley Ball coerced Lydia to take a walk with him in order to keep their business private. Once in a suitable place he simply cut her throat then buried the body in a shallow grave in a ditch, making it virtually impossible to locate her body. With no body and no real witnesses he was relatively certain to escape judgement, though perhaps after all judgement was served upon him by the conduct and attitudes of those who always knew him to be guilty.

Locally a ballad was produced titled *The Cruel Butcher of Ringstead*. It consisted of eight damning verses with reference to Weekley Ball, the chorus being –

'O, cruel butcher, he hung should be
For the killing of Lydia Atley!'

# THE
# CORPSE
# IN THE BOXROOM

S ELDOM do official authorities feel any sympathy for a self-confessed killer. But in 1938 Northamptonshire was the setting for a crime which aroused so much local sympathy towards a killer that it easily stands out from the average act of murder. The facts of the case are based around the town of Higham Ferrers, which is situated approximately five miles from Kettering in East Northants.

Wharf Road, Higham Ferrers was and still is a pleasant area in which to reside. There is nothing special about the road, indeed it is similar to hundreds of thousands of others all over the United Kingdom, yet Wharf Road is unique in many respects as murder occurred within its boundaries. Number 92 is situated close to the bottom of a slight incline and was in 1938 a typical family home. The couple who resided there were Albert Hedley Harrison and his wife Mabel Annie Harrison, with their two sons Keith and Clifford.

The couple had married in 1918 and had resided in North Street, Raunds prior to moving to Higham Ferrers some time around 1936. Mabel Harrison had been connected with the Salvation Army since an early age when she attended the Salvation

Albert Hedley Harrison and Mabel Harrison. 'Mild mannered' Harrison resorted to murder when he could no longer endure his wife's infidelities.

Army Sunday school at Wellingborough. Albert Hedley Harrison worked as a shoe operative for Messrs R. Coggins & Sons Ltd of Raunds. He was by all accounts a pleasant and mild mannered 42 year old. Mabel Harrison also worked in the shoe trade at Wright's, Higham Ferrers. She was one year younger than her husband and possessed a completely different personality to him. She was seemingly dominant, though it may be the case that her husband allowed her such dominance in preference to confrontation. To all intents and purposes the couple were quite content with their lot and went about their business in a normal manner.

It was at 9.50 am on Saturday 20th August 1938 when Albert Harrison left his home in Wharf Road. It was a pleasant sort of morning in the town, which was hard at work preparing for the annual Feast Day celebrations and people could be seen busying themselves for the occasion. Albert Harrison climbed on his bicycle and rode through Higham Ferrers and down into the town area of nearby Rushden, where his destination was the police station. Harrison calmly entered the station office area and requested to speak with the Duty Inspector.

Within moments Harrison was ushered into Inspector Valentine's office and said, 'You are the Inspector? I expect you will soon be wanting me. I wish to tell you that I strangled my wife last night.' The Inspector was somewhat surprised by the man's comments and carefully explained to him the seriousness of such statements. He then cautioned Harrison and instructed a fellow officer to record his personal details.

In the meantime the Inspector contacted Doctor O.A.J.N. Muriset of Rushden and requested that he attend at the house as a precaution. The Inspector must have been slightly perturbed at Harrison's cool manner and cannot have imagined any such incident occurring in Higham Ferrers!

A key to the house was procured from Harrison and the Inspector, accompanied by other uniformed police officers, attended the Harrison home. Bloodstains were found in the hall and on the staircase bannister, further smears were located upon the kitchen door. It seemed clear that some form of violent struggle had taken place within the home but there was no sign of Mabel Harrison's body. On climbing the stairs the group found a small wooden door which had been sealed and secured by two nails. The nails were removed and the door opened. Within the tiny area lay the body of Mabel Annie Harrison. The corpse had been covered by a white bed sheet, which was removed. The doctor and the Inspector observed a stained white bootlace secured tightly around the dead woman's neck. This had cut into the skin. Her face bore the signs of a violent confrontation, with numerous cuts evident upon her cheeks. There were also signs of contusions. What was more curious was the fact that the dead woman's hands were white as though they had been scrubbed clean. Bloodstained clothing lay beside the body and this bore the appearance of having been thrust into the tiny room in a great hurry. The Inspector could hardly believe the scene nor the fact that the killer was locked away in a police cell prior to the locating of a body!

A police constable was detailed to stand guard at the house in order to prevent access to any unauthorised persons. The house was sealed off as inquisitive neighbours wondered just what had occurred within number 92. Inspector Valentine returned to Rushden police station and briefed Superintendent Williams of the situation, with the latter immediately informing Harrison that he was under arrest on suspicion of murdering his wife. The house in Wharf Road underwent detailed examination which provided a further clue, a second white bootlace was found in a football boot situated in an outhouse. A few hours later the police satisfied themselves that all the evidence had been located and thus departed the house, leaving neighbours guessing as to the purpose of their enquiries. The area had little longer to wait before they witnessed a body being removed from the house and the talk was soon of murder. The body was taken to Wellingborough police station mortuary where it was identified later that same afternoon by Mr Abraham Cooke of Chelmsford, father of the dead woman.

A special court hearing was held in Higham Ferrers town hall that afternoon requesting authorisation for Harrison to remain in police custody pending further police enquiries. The news of the crime had spread through the town and into Rushden, yet no one knew of Albert Harrison's whereabouts except those police officers involved in the enquiry. An unmarked police car drew up outside the police station and Albert Hedley Harrison appeared shortly afterwards flanked by a plain clothes police officer. He appeared to be rather aloof to his surroundings. The car travelled to Higham Ferrers town hall. On arrival the streets were deserted and music filled the air along with the screams and squeals of children enjoying themselves at the nearby pleasure fair, which was in the town for its celebrations. The hearing lasted but a few minutes. Harrison was remanded and left the proceedings as quietly as he had arrived, being driven to Wellingborough police station for further in-depth questioning.

The questioning provided an accurate account of the crime

which proved to be influential in the subsequent court hearing. The statement read: 'I was married to my wife on August 3rd 1918, at Raunds. My wife and I lived at North Street, Raunds before moving to Wharf Road. During the time we were living at Raunds, my wife's name was coupled with that of another man, about twelve years ago.

'About six years ago her name was again mentioned as going out with the same man, and one night I found the same man in my house. I accused the same man and my wife of associating together, but both denied it, and these happenings caused trouble between myself and my wife. About two years ago I and my wife came to live in Wharf Road, Higham Ferrers, and about three months later my wife started work at Messrs Wrights in the same town, earning about 30 shillings per week. During the last few months she used to go out Friday and Saturday nights, and said that on Saturdays she went out with a lady friend, sometimes to Raunds.

'I believed my wife's visits were perfectly harmless until on Thursday August 18th a Mrs Talbot of Raunds, came to see me at my work and stated that her husband had been going out with my wife for the past twelve months. She had searched her husband's pockets and found certain articles in them. She then asked if she could come over to my house that night to see my wife. She came that night and accused my wife of associating with her husband, which she denied. The man Talbot worked at the same factory as my wife and used to see her alone at 1.10 pm each day. That same night I searched Raunds for Talbot but could not find him.'

It was obvious to investigating officials that the news broken to Albert Harrison by Mrs Talbot was devastating. He had later searched the village of Raunds for his wife's lover, initially, one may assume, to serve out some form of physical punishment to Talbot. In fact, Harrison was simply attempting to confirm the illicit liaison. The statement continued to reveal a deep insight into the problems encountered by a loyal and devoted husband and father:

'On Friday the 19th August I got up at 6.15 am to see my boy off to work. My wife got up at 7.30 am and cut some lunch for herself, she then went to work. I did not go to work that day as I felt very much upset but I went to Raunds and asked a mate to collect my wages for me. My wife came home at 5.30 pm. I had a kettle of boiling water on the gas. My wife emptied it into a jug and said, "I am going to see him tonight". I believe she meant Talbot. I said "You are not". With that she tried to throw boiling water over me, I dodged it. She then started to run upstairs and fell upon the bottom step, striking her eye, and started shouting abuse at me. I went for her and she must have turned round as she scratched my face on the left side, and while she lay there I put my hands around her neck. She did not struggle much, and I pulled a lace from my pocket and tied it around her neck. I was very much upset at the time and could not have been responsible for my actions as I loved my wife and there was no other woman in the world for me.

'By this time it was around 6.30 pm. I carried her to what we call the boxroom. I saw there was some blood on the stair carpet, bannister and a little on the wall. I washed it off as well as I could with some clothing which I put in the boxroom. Feeling sure that my wife was dead I nailed up the door so that my boy should not go in. I then washed and changed my clothes, locked up the house and went to Rushden to meet my mate with my wages. I left home at about 7.30 pm, meeting my mate at 8 pm, with whom I went for a drink of beer in the Wheatsheaf public house. I bought a quartern of whisky and a small bottle of beer to take home with me. I returned home after collecting my son from the fair, and we went to bed sleeping in separate rooms. My son never asked where his mother was.

'The next morning I got up at 5.30 am, got my boy's breakfast and later came to Rushden police station and told the police what I had done.'

Albert Harrison was brought before a further special hearing at Higham Ferrers town hall. On that occasion the streets were lined with sightseers and friends of the family, all gathered in the hope of catching a glimpse of the man who had caused the county's biggest sensation for eight years. The unmarked police car containing Harrison slipped in and out of the rear access point to the hall encountering few obstacles. The mood of the crowd was incredible. Almost all supported Albert Harrison and objected to his probable imprisonment.

Such was the public interest in the case that his friends and colleagues grouped together and requested subscriptions to assist with the financing of a reasonable defence counsel for the accused. Some 7,000 subscriptions were received, thus providing financial aid to support the hiring of one of the greatest defence lawyers this country has ever known, Norman Birkett KC.

Local talk was of Mabel Harrison's adulterous affairs. Public opinion seemed to favour the husband though there were those whose loyalties still remained with the dead woman. Mabel Harrison's funeral took place on Wednesday 24th August 1938 at the Wellingborough-Doddington Road cemetery. Some 800 persons were in attendance; most were work colleagues but others were the typical curiosity seekers. Various wreaths and sentimental items were placed upon the coffin including a heart-rendering verse from her parents. Mabel Harrison was buried with great respect, one noticeable absentee being her husband!

Some two months later, on Friday 21st October 1938, Albert Hedley Harrison was brought to trial at Northampton assizes, presiding judge Mr Justice Oliver. Harrison entered the dock at precisely 11.19 am wearing a smart deep blue suit and a black tie. Theatrically, a bowl of red roses stood in the middle of the courtroom. Every so often shafts of strong golden sunlight shone through the courthouse windows directly onto the roses, giving the impression that they were drawing power from the illuminating rays.

Albert Harrison pleaded not guilty to the charge of murder; a plea thoroughly supported by some of those present in the court room. Mr Maurice Healy, prosecuting barrister, was exceedingly lenient in his case for the Crown. It was, he deliberated, 'an accepted fact that the woman met her death by a deliberate – deliberate in one sense – act of the accused, and a voluntary act that having strangled her with his hands, he made doubly sure by tying a lace round her neck. In this case there might be contentions made that he killed her in such circumstances as would justify them in reducing the verdict to one of manslaughter.'

The prosecuting barrister continued to expound upon Albert Harrison's excellent and impeccable character. He told the court sympathetically of 'the considerable element of pathos.' Soon everyone within that courtroom realised that Albert Hedley Harrison was the unfortunate victim of circumstances. He had dearly loved his wife and family and provided for their every need, only to have such actions abused by his wife. Albert Harrison knew some six years previous to his court appearance that his wife was being unfaithful, yet he had bravely (or stupidly) ignored such hurtful incidents.

Norman Birkett KC then took to the floor proffering his case for the defence. The speech by Birkett proved to be so emotional that it actually brought Harrison to tears. The defence counsel explained to the court that he would allow his client to plead guilty to manslaughter but in no way could he be deemed guilty of murder. He added that, from all the evidence, he had perceived manslaughter was the correct and only charge acceptable. Mr Justice Oliver requested the Crown to offer any objection to this point, none was forthcoming and the Crown agreed with the defence counsel. Birkett ended his defence speech, 'The man realises and recognises that there must be punishment. In one sense no punishment that you, your Lordship, could inflict could ever be heavier than the punishment that this man now bears. The remorse, the contrition, will remain with him for all time. All I can do is to say here is a tragic and sad case, the law itself is merciful, but over and above that mercy is the prerogative of this court, and I ask

Tranquil Wharf Road today looking much as it did in 1938, when the violent murder of Mabel Harrison shocked its suburban serenity.

you, having regard to your public duty and the unique circumstances, to treat this man mercifully and as leniently as you can. It is not a case where deterrent is concerned. I commend this unfortunate man to your Lordship's most merciful consideration.'

Mr Justice Oliver himself seemed highly moved by Birkett's remarkable plea. Making his closing and final speech the judge said, 'It seems terrible to me to prolong an investigation of this sort which can only have one result. I am weak enough to wish that the task of dealing with you had fallen on to any judge but me, there are circumstances for which you are not in the least to be blamed and over which you had no control, but I am bound to administer the law. I have weighed every word your counsel has said – there is no man at the Bar who could have said it better. The least I can possibly sentence you to is three years penal servitude.'

Albert Harrison broke down and wept in gratitude for his brilliant defending counsel, who without doubt plucked him from the shadow of the gallows. Just 66 minutes after entering the courtroom, Albert Hedley Harrison left to begin his punishment.

In all my years of research into the crime of murder I have never encountered such an emotive trial where all official parties display such sympathy. Whether you agree or disagree with the verdict is a matter of opinion, seldom can there be such courtroom deliberations. When compared to other classic cases, the most obvious being that of Doctor Crippen, who also murdered his wife, one must consider Harrison fortunate. The only real difference between the cases is that Harrison openly confessed his crime and gave himself up without further conflict, Crippen attempted to escape. Both were married to so-called 'unfaithful women' who were of a stronger will and personality and although Crippen hanged for his crime, undoubtedly Harrison suffered greater mental anguish for his!

# THE
# MURDERS OF
# BARTON SEAGRAVE

THERE are two Northamptonshire murders of some historical note, one of which has become a popular legend in
more recent years. The legend is a remarkably accurate
account of the factual data. There can surely be no other tale of
murder occurring in such atrocious weather conditions, or which
displays so dramatically how the wrath of one human being could
eventually destroy everything he treasured.

Barton Seagrave is situated some two miles south-east of Kettering. It is now quite an average sized community but chooses to
retain its village status rather than be classed as a town. A fair
amount of the old village still stands close to St Botolph's church,
near the original village green. Immediately opposite the green
(across Polwell Lane) stands a row of beautiful thatched cottages
which back onto an undulating field. In this field once stood
Barton Seagrave castle, on a site which is now known locally as the
'Hilly Hollies'. The undulations in this field are in fact the founda-
tions of the old castle which has now disappeared from public
view, being engulfed by grass and wild flowers.

In the 14th century the castle was owned by Lord Nicolas De
Segrave (minus the 'a'). De Segrave was by all accounts a domi-

nant person who did not suffer fools gladly. He had made many enemies through his less than sympathetic attitude towards his village workers, many of whom resented him. An avid royalist, Nicolas De Segrave did everything his King asked of him and relied upon no man, that is until he saw the beauty of a local girl with whom he fell passionately in love.

De Segrave was returning from battle and was passing through Latimer (now Burton Latimer) when he caught sight of Lady Isabel Latimer, daughter of Lord Latimer of the neighbouring village. There was much animosity between these men. Lord Latimer was a totally different type of person. He cared for his workforce and often rewarded them for their loyalty and hard work, and in response to this he possessed much in the way of respect from all those who worked for him. Latimer and De Segrave had resented each other for many years. The obvious personality differences were the main agitators, but undoubtedly De Segrave's supercilious demeanour did not enhance matters. Latimer was of a different political background and found himself in personal disagreement with much of what the King did. Sensibly he maintained silence about such opinions, but one can see that there was little that these men could agree upon.

De Segrave rode back to his castle with the image of Lady Isabel engraved upon his mind. Never before had he seen such a ravishing beauty and he found it difficult to understand how one so beautiful could be the daughter of Lord Latimer, but he realised there was little he could do to alter this.

Deviously De Segrave elected to grovel to Lord Latimer in the hope that he might be able to sway Lady Isabel into marriage. He falsely believed that this would be an easy task to accomplish but underestimated his counterpart. Sending a rider to Lord Latimer's home with a personal note, De Segrave requested that both men meet to resolve their differences and sent his kindest wishes to Lady Isabel. Lord Latimer was unimpressed and sent the rider away with a negative reply in response to De Segrave's request.

Nicolas De Segrave was furious and swore to achieve his objective of marrying Lady Isabel. For many weeks the local feud increased in fury, though no physical incidents occurred until De Segrave made his decisive move. Late one evening he saw Lady Isabel out walking alone. Approaching her on his horse he bade her a good evening and stopped to talk. With Lady Isabel relaxed, he suddenly bent down and hauled her onto the back of his mount and galloped off to his castle. On arrival there he attempted to coerce Lady Isabel into marrying him but all such requests were denied by the frightened woman, who explained that she was betrothed to another, namely one Hugh Neville, another local man in Latimer's area.

De Segrave was furious, as his spies had failed to advise him of this obstacle (for reasons better kept to themselves). He ordered that Lady Isabel be locked in the castle dungeons at once where she would be tended by a young servant boy. Every so often De Segrave would visit Lady Isabel in her cell in the dank dark dungeons, and each time he did so he would leave enraged by the girl's resilience. Unbeknown to De Segrave, the young servant boy had actually befriended Lady Isabel and had fallen under her charm; he frequently passed secret messages to Hugh Neville and Lord Latimer.

Through this contact Hugh Neville was able to manipulate the boy into releasing Lady Isabel into his arms. Nicolas De Segrave had left the castle on business elsewhere within the county, and he had been gone for some time before Neville and his brother appeared. The night was indeed dark, the skies were full of thunder and heavy rain, every so often the castle would tremble as thunder rolled around its walls and bolts of lightning struck out, illuminating its darkest recesses. The young boy must have thought that the Devil was attempting to punish him for releasing Lady Isabel back into the arms of her genuine loved one. Hugh Neville placed Lady Isabel on the back of his horse and trotted towards the river Ise where he could cross and make good his escape. As the pair approached the river a flash of lightning lit up the fields on the opposite side of the river. Neville must have shivered as the sudden flash showed the silhouette of a great ghastly form on horseback on the opposite bank. It was Nicolas De Segrave. Another flash of lightning glinted off shiny metal, De Segrave had drawn his sword. Quickly Neville allowed Lady Isabel to dismount. De Segrave too had dismounted and was walking towards Neville, who called to him to come to his senses.

De Segrave was past hearing. He approached Lady Isabel and with a quick movement slashed her throat, killing her instantly. Enraged, Hugh Neville leapt upon De Segrave and the men fought a wicked battle during an horrific thunder and lightning storm. De Segrave overcame his attacker and similarly slit Hugh Neville's

The approximate site of the 14th century murder of Hugh Neville and Lady Isabel. As the lovers attempted to cross the river Ise, a flash of lightning revealed the villainous Nicolas De Segrave awaiting them.

throat before riding back to the castle. There he cut the young servant boy's throat for being so disobedient. Nicolas De Segrave escaped any real punishment and denied the crime, though most people knew he had killed the lovers. Curiously De Segrave died shortly after the incident, though the cause of death is unknown. It is claimed within the legend that Lady Isabel swore to haunt him, after he had cut her throat and before she disappeared into the murky depths of the then fast flowing river Ise. The legend continues that every so often Lady Isabel returned to the castle and eventually her killer died of a broken heart after he realised what beauty he had destroyed! The scene of the alarming confrontation on the Ise still exists though not in any form which any one of these characters could now recognise. Each bank of the river is now bridged, which stands on the busy A6 road into Kettering, and the river itself is little more than a narrow stream hardly wide enough for two men to stand in. There are those who claim to have sighted a ghostly apparition floating/skimming across these waters on a darkened night. This they believe is the wandering spirit of Lady Isabel searching for her slaughtered lover!

The second curious tale of murder also revolves around the community of Barton Seagrave, though this time upon the quaint village green where once it is claimed stood a coaching inn. The inn was ideally situated along the routes north and south and one can imagine must have been highly profitable. Sometime around the late 1600s a violent confrontation took place within the inn between two travelling men. This in itself was not unique as such violence was and is all too common in similar environments. What is interesting about this particular quarrel is that it continued outside the inn and resulted in a duel which would end in death for one traveller. The confrontation was witnessed by a number of people and seemed as if it might continue for many hours dependent upon the strength and build of each aggressor. The crowd of onlookers soon became bored and tired of the confrontation and elected to return to the peace and relative tranquillity of the inn.

Some time later one of the men entered the inn and was given a rapturous welcome. Drinks were avidly consumed and no one spared a thought for the unfortunate individual who had been killed in the duel. The night wore on and the following morning before daylight the inn emptied and its visitors departed for their destinations.

The innkeeper rose early and it was just after daylight when he noted a stranger standing by a tree on the village green. He bid the man a good morning but received no reply. Later he again saw the man standing by the same tree and this time decided to ascertain what his business was. On approaching the tree the innkeeper received the shock of his life. The man was actually impaled to the tree and was pinned by virtue of a sword having been thrust through his middle and deep into the heart of the tree. No one knew the man's identity, nor his killer's, who was to become something of a folklore hero of superhuman strength in latter years.

# INDEX

INDEX